THE COMPLETE GUIDE TO AKITAS

Erin Hotovy

Publication Data

Akitas

The Complete Guide to Akitas – First edition.

Summary: "Successfully raising an Akita Dog from puppy to old age" – Provided by publisher.

ISBN: 978-1-952069-92-5

[1. Akitas – Non-Fiction] I. Title.

Design by Sorin Rădulescu

First paperback edition, 2020

TABLE OF CONTENTS

CHAPTER 1

Akita Basics 1
What is an Akita? 1
The History of the Akita 3
The Akita in America 4
Physical Characteristics 6
Is an Akita the Right Fit for You? 6

CHAPTER 2

Choosing an Akita 9
Buying vs. Adopting 9
How to Find a Reputable Breeder 11
Researching Breeders 13
Health Tests, Certifications, and Breeder Guarantees 14
Choosing the Perfect Pup 16

CHAPTER 3

Preparing Your Home for Your Akita 17
The Protective Akita 18
Preparing Your Family and Your Pets 18
Preparing Your Home 20
Getting Your Yard Ready for Your Akita 23
Necessary Supplies for Your Akita 24

CHAPTER 4

Bringing Your Akita Home 27
The Importance of Having a Plan 28
The Ride Home 28
The First Night Home 29

Keeping Your Akita Comfortable at the Vet 32

Cost Breakdown for the First Year 34

CHAPTER 5

Being a Puppy Parent **37**

Setting Realistic Expectations 38

Common Puppy Problems 40

Biting 41

Chewing 41

Accidents 41

Jumping Up 42

Separation Anxiety 43

CHAPTER 6

Potty Training **45**

Being Consistent 46

Options for Potty Training 46

Keeping it Positive 48

Potty Training an Adult Akita 49

Crates, Playpens, and Doggy Doors 50

CHAPTER 7

Socializing with People and Animals **53**

Greeting New Human Friends 54

Socializing with Other Dogs 56

Socializing with Other Animals 59

Pack Mentality 60

Raising Multiple Akitas 62

CHAPTER 8

Physical and Mental Exercise **63**

Exercise Requirements 64

Activities to Do with Your Akita 65

Mental Exercise 68

CHAPTER 9

Training Your Akita 71

Setting Clear Expectations 72

Using Operant Conditioning 73

The Best Reinforcements for Your Akita 74

Training with Positivity 76

Hiring a Trainer 76

CHAPTER 10

Commands 79

Basic Commands 80

    Sit 80

    Down 81

    Stay 82

    Come 82

    Off 84

    Drop It 84

Walk 85

Advanced Commands 87

    Take it/Leave it 87

    Shake/High Five 87

    Crawl 88

    Spin 88

CHAPTER 11

Traveling with Your Akita 89

Dog Crates and Car Restraints 90

Preparing Your Dog for Car Rides 91

Flying and Hotel Stays 94

Kenneling vs. Dog Sitters 96

Tips and Tricks for Traveling 97

CHAPTER 12

Nutrition **99**
Importance of a Good Diet 100
Choosing a Commercial Dog Food 102
Cooking for Your Akita 104
Feeding Table Scraps 106
Treats 107
Weight Management 107

CHAPTER 13

Grooming Your Akita **109**
Coat Basics 110
Managing Your Akita's Coat Blow 110
Bath Time 111
Trimming Toenails 113
Brushing Teeth 114
Cleaning Ears and Eyes 116

CHAPTER 14

Basic Health Care **117**
Fleas and Ticks 117
Worms and Internal Parasites 119
Supplements and Natural Health Care 122
Vaccinations 123
Pet Insurance 124
Genetic Health of Akitas 125

CHAPTER 15

Your Aging Akita **127**
Caring for Your Aging Akita 128
When It's Time to Say Goodbye 133

CHAPTER 1

Akita Basics

What is an Akita?

The Akita is a sturdy, double-coated dog that originates from Japan. Once favored as fierce hunters, today's society sees Akitas as companions and as protectors of family. Their playful personality adds to the loyalty they have for their owner. However, do not be surprised if this breed is not interested in associating with strangers or other animals; they can be wary of unknown people and places, and they are sometimes aggressive

Photo Courtesy of Charlie Pound

*Photo Courtesy
of Gustavo Lomeli*

toward other dogs, especially of the same sex. These tendencies can be rectified with socialization and with positive reinforcement if begun as a puppy.

There are two recognized varieties of Akita—the Japanese Akita, or Akita-Inu, and the Akita bred in America. While these dogs come from the same initial stock, there are some significant differences in how they have developed, most obviously in size. Japanese-variety Akitas typically weigh in at around 55-75 pounds; those bred in America are a bit larger, usually between 70-130 pounds. There are also small differences in eye shape, the positioning of the ears, and the width of the skull.

Neither variety of Akita is small enough to make a good lapdog, though they may try and convince you otherwise. These are smart, active companions, who take well to consistent and training, but without proper training, they can become disrespectful and difficult to control.

This chapter supplies information on the Akita breed, so you can make a knowledgeable decision on whether or not this is the right breed of dog for you. Once you have determined an Akita will be a great addition to your family, you will find the remainder of this book to be a step-by-step guide for caring for this incredible breed!

The History of the Akita

This is one of the oldest-known dog breeds, developed several hundred years ago from native Japanese dogs called Matagi-Inu. Akitas, named for the Akita prefecture in Japan where they originated, were employed as hunting dogs and property guardians as early as the 1500s. These powerful, fearless dogs were particularly adept at hunting large game, including boar, elk, and Japanese black bear. As hunting declined in the nineteenth century, these majestic animals were often relegated to fighting in dog fights. The beginning of the twentieth century in Japan brought war, rabies outbreaks, and famine, causing canine populations to drop dramatically, especially in large, fur-bearing dogs such as the Akita.

It was during this troubled time that Hachikō, perhaps the most famous of all Akitas, was acquired by Hidesaburō Ueno, a professor at Tokyo Imperial University. Hachikō was a loyal pet who faithfully accompanied his owner to the train station each morning, then returned to escort him home in the late afternoon. One day in May 1925, Professor Ueno suffered a brain hemorrhage while teaching. Although Hachikō's owner never returned, the loyal canine continued returning to the station at 3 p.m. every afternoon, hoping to meet his beloved owner. It was a vigil the dog kept for nearly a decade until he passed away in March 1935. Today, several statues of Hachikō commemorate the loyal dog in Japan, and his story has been shared with the rest of the world through books, television, and film.

The Akita in America

On a visit to Japan in the late 1930s, Helen Keller visited the Akita district in Japan after hearing the story of Hachikō. She was enamored by the breed's loyalty, and during her visit, she was gifted an Akita puppy of her own. Helen's pup, Kamikaze-Go, and his successor, Kenzan-Go, were the only known Akita breed dogs residing in America until the end of World War II. American soldiers that had been stationed in Japan during World War II returned with Akitas, and the breed's popularity grew.

In the 1950s, Akitas were bred on American soil for the first time, but American breeders and Japanese breeders had differing opinions on what the ideal Akita should look like. American breeders favored larger dogs with wider, bear-like heads as guard dogs. Japanese breeders, in an attempt to recreate the standards of the original Akita, preferred a more lightly built frame with a fox-like face. The differences between the two were substantial enough for the UKC, AKC, and FCI to each list separate breed standards for both the American and the Japanese varieties of Akita.

Photo Courtesy
of Nathanael Wilson

Physical Characteristics

Akitas are large dogs that stand between 24 and 28 inches tall and have stout, muscular bodies. Like many cold-weather breeds, they have a typical Spitz-type appearance, with erect, triangular ears, pointed muzzles, and bushy tails that curl up over their backs. They tend to have a regal and dignified bearing with a confident, powerful gait.

The Akita prefecture, where this breed was developed, is near the northern tip of Honshū island—a cold northern region characterized by tall, snowy mountains. Akitas have thick, bushy coats with a dense layer of soft underfur to protect them from the freezing temperatures and bitter winds. Their coat comes in a wide variety of colors and patterns. Akitas of any color are acceptable by American breed standards, but Japanese Akita standards are restricted to white, red fawn, brindle, and sesame. The dogs often have "masks," which is when their face is a different color than their predominant coat color, and most sport urajiro markings, a white or cream color on the underside of the jaw, neck, chest, and belly, as well as the sides of the muzzles and the inside of the legs.

While Akitas do have a thick, abundant coat, they don't typically require as much grooming as other dogs with a similar coat. These dogs are known for their fastidiousness and often spend a great deal of time grooming themselves.

Is an Akita the Right Fit for You?

Before bringing home a new puppy or an adult Akita, you should decide if you are ready to take care of an Akita for the rest of his life. All dog breeds are different and with distinct personalities, and Akitas are no exception. If you find that you are not prepared to take care of a breed with this background or temperament, it does NOT mean you cannot give a different breed of dog a great home.

Sometimes dogs are placed in shelters because their owner realized they could not handle the dog's specific needs. This makes it difficult to find a loving home for a wonderful dog that simply needs a capable owner. So, take a look at your home, your finances, and your lifestyle before making this major commitment.

Perhaps the most important thing to consider before bringing home an Akita is who is already living in your household. If you live alone, have a partner, or live with roommates, an Akita may be a great fit because this breed loves the comfort of a family.

FUN FACT
Akita Club of America (ACA)

The Akita Club of America (ACA) was founded as a nonprofit in 1960 and is the only American Kennel Club (AKC) Parent Club for Akitas in America. The ACA hosts an annual meeting and Annual National Specialty Show. Like other parent clubs, the ACA's primary objective is the preservation and protection of the Akita breed. More information can be found on their website: www.akitaclub.org

They are good around children, but as with any dog, some Akitas can become nervous around young, excitable children. On the other hand, older children will keep your Akita entertained and will prevent him from becoming lonely.

If your family members include other pets, you may find that an Akita may NOT be the right addition to your crew. For instance, Akitas have a high prey drive, which means they sometimes get the urge to chase a cat or other small animal. They can, however, be socialized to get along with other dogs, but they are not known for being overly "dog friendly." If you have no other pets and are planning to bring only one Akita into your home, then you can rest assured this breed will be a loving addition to your home!

You should also consider how much time you have to dedicate to an Akita. This breed of dog is not happy if they are expected to spend a lot of time home alone. Akitas also require a lot of exercise and entertaining, so you must be willing to commit several hours a day giving them your undivided attention. You must spend enough time at home with your dog, so he does not feel he has been abandoned.

Next, consider the experience you have with raising a dog. Akitas can be stubborn and display behaviors that may be too much for a novice dog owner to handle. If you have never raised a dog or lived in a household with a dog, owning an Akita may be a big and frightening first step! However, this book will give you the tools you need to learn about caring for an Akita and to feel comfortable around your new best friend!

With any breed of dog, it is important to consider the financial commitment you are about to make. The Akita is generally no more expensive to raise than the average dog breed, but costs do add up over time.

The initial cost of an Akita puppy can be around a thousand dollars, and then you have to consider all of the other necessary costs! Caring for a dog includes a lot of supplies: dog food, training treats, leashes, vaccinations, preventative medicine, and toys...to name a few. Plus, you might want to enroll your pup in training classes, and what about regular appointments with the veterinarian? You will have to adjust your budget to include these added expenses; if you know unexpected, dog-related bills will put you in a tough financial position, consider waiting until you have more savings. The relationship with your new best friend deserves a solid beginning!

Rushing into dog ownership is never a good idea. A new owner spends a lot of time, energy, attention, and money on their dog in order to keep him happy and healthy. If you find yourself unable to provide for an Akita now, it is best to wait until your circumstances change. It is easy to get excited about buying an Akita puppy, but it is in everyone's best interest to make sure you are able to provide your dog with everything he needs.

If you have decided that your next step is to definitely buy an Akita puppy, keep reading! The following chapters will guide you through the purchasing process and give you step-by-step instruction for how to care for a little puppy.

CHAPTER 2

Choosing an Akita

Buying vs. Adopting

Buying an Akita puppy from a breeder has its advantages. First, if you buy from a reputable breeder, you know exactly what kind of dog you will be purchasing. Physical and behavioral characteristics can be bred, so if you like the puppy's parents, you'll probably like the puppy. For example, if you're looking for an intelligent and playful pup, you'll want to ensure that the parents show those qualities. Similarly, if the parents are aggressive or nervous, those characteristics may be passed on to the offspring.

Also, when purchasing a puppy from a breeder, you are able to "start from scratch"; this means you will know that your pup has been well cared for by the breeder – from birth to the time leading up to your purchase.

Finally, if you expect to find an Akita puppy in a rescue shelter (instead of buying from a breeder), you might be disappointed because Akita puppies in shelters can be hard to come by!

Photo Courtesy of Laura Storer

On the other hand, you can most definitely adopt a fantastic Akita adult from a shelter. Adopting an adult Akita and offering a loving home as a place to begin again is an extremely rewarding feeling! Adopting an adult dog can also save you time and energy when it comes to training. It takes a lot of work to housetrain a new puppy, but sometimes adopted dogs are already housetrained, and some even know basic obedience skills.

Adoption fees are a fraction of the cost of buying a puppy, and adult dogs tend to be more mild-mannered than energetic puppies. So, if you aren't sure you can handle the work and time commitment of raising a puppy, you might find yourself just as excited about adopting an adult Akita!

If you decide to adopt your Akita, make sure you do your research first. For example, some animal shelters and rescues care for a mix of breeds or a mix of different animals. Other rescue shelters are breed-specific and focus on finding homes for one or two certain breeds of dog. Both types will be helpful in finding the perfect Akita for your family but be sure you talk with the volunteers and workers before making a commitment.

The first question to ask is why the Akita was put up for adoption. You may find the dog did not get along well in a certain home or simply that the owner could not commit to the time it takes to care for an Akita. By knowing this information, you can avoid bringing an Akita into a home with cats (or other small pets) if that was the reason he was brought into the shelter in the first place!

With adoption, it is hard to know how the dog will behave in your home. More often than not, rescues end up in shelters because the owners could not care for the dog - not because the dog had problems. However, there are some cases in which an Akita might be surrendered because he did not get along with other pets or children. This information is vital before choosing to bring an Akita to your already large family!

You might also negotiate an introductory period with your rescue center. Before making the adoption permanent, you might want to introduce the dog to your family and to any other pets. Not only will you be assured the adoption is a good fit for you and your family, but this will give the rescue time to examine your home and your yard to determine if the new environment is safe and "dog-ready." They will also check with your references to ensure that you are able to cater to an Akita's needs.

If you decide to adopt an adult Akita, and you pass the rescue's standards, you will likely have to pay a small adoption fee. Fortunately, this amount usually covers the cost of vaccinations, veterinarian care, neutering, and training; plus, the cost helps keep the shelter open for other animals in need. Not a big price to pay when you know your adoption fee is helping other animals that may be struggling and homeless.

How to Find a Reputable Breeder

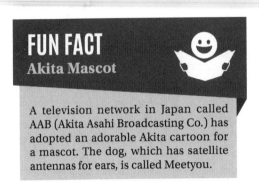

FUN FACT
Akita Mascot

A television network in Japan called AAB (Akita Asahi Broadcasting Co.) has adopted an adorable Akita cartoon for a mascot. The dog, which has satellite antennas for ears, is called Meetyou.

If you decide you want to buy an Akita puppy from a breeder, it is important to find the right pup. Anyone can breed and sell dogs, but that does not mean you should buy a puppy from just any-one. Buying from a reputable breeder helps preserve the best qualities of a breed, gives business to people who are experts in Akita care, and ensures that you will own a healthy dog, one that has been very well cared for by the breeder.

Novice dog breeders can range from inexperienced (but well meaning) to downright dangerous and dishonest. If an Akita breeder is not an expert in all things Akita, he or she may not know how to properly breed dogs or know what characteristics are favored in this breed.

Unfortunately, genetic diseases can be bred into a litter of pups if the breeder does not have the appropriate knowledge, which can lead to sick puppies, high vet bills for new owners, and heartbreak for your family. Some breeders are more concerned about the money they make from selling popular puppy breeds than they do about properly caring for their dogs. These operations are often referred to as "puppy mills" because they are only concerned with producing puppies, like in a factory or a "mill", and they keep their dogs in dirty, cramped quarters not caring about the health and wellbeing of their animals. Not only do you want to avoid buying a puppy from an inexperienced or bad breeder, but you also do not want to support their business.

If you do not know where to look for a reputable Akita breeder, talk with people who know dogs. Veterinarians, dog trainers, kennel club organiza-tions, and other Akita owners might be able to make recommendations. An internet search will also yield some results, but it can be hard sifting through information without a frame of reference. Try to gather names of a few different breeders, then begin a researching and vetting process to make sure you have found a breeder you are comfortable with – someone you can trust.

Photo Courtesy
of Marissa Nowlan

Researching Breeders

An easy first step in researching your narrowed-down list of breeders is to look at the breeders' websites or social media pages. A reputable breeder will post their credentials in a prominent place on their website, which will likely include involvement in Akita organizations and with show-winning dogs. If a website has useful information about Akitas, it shows the breeder is knowledgeable about the breed and is interested in sharing this knowledge with others. It is also helpful if your breeder has a social media page with posts from satisfied customers; these comments might answer questions you have and reassure your feelings about the breeder.

When interviewing each breeder, ask if you can visit their facility and see their dogs. Be mindful many breeders operate out of their home, so they may not want visitors at all hours of the day! However, they should

Photo Courtesy of Stiina Juhanson

still be flexible and accommodating; be wary of a breeder that does not let clients see their dogs or their breeding operations because they may have something to hide. If you visit a breeder and their kennel is cramped, dirty, or smells bad, this could indicate they do not care for their dogs properly. If the dogs are not kept in sanitary conditions, the breeder is likely not working with champion stock. Walk away from these situations!

Finally, look for a breeder who wants to keep in touch with you after the sale is finalized. A good breeder, one who cares about their pups, will want to help you through the early days of life with your dog and to be sure your Akita is happy and adjusts to his new home. If your breeder does not want to be contacted after selling you a pup, it might be because they do not want to deal with potential complaints. Again, walk away from these breeders – they are not the loving, caring people who have your dog's best interest at heart.

After researching and collecting as much information as possible about your potential breeder, you may need to wait until the puppies are available...and that's okay! Do not rush to buy the first available pup just because you are eager to bring home a dog. Wait until the right dog for you and your family is available...you will be so much happier!

Health Tests, Certifications, and Breeder Guarantees

One thing that separates a reputable, experienced breeder from a puppy mill is their ability to prove their knowledge and their expertise with dog breeding. An excellent breeder has nothing to hide when it comes to their puppies; they know their dogs are healthy and have all of the wonderful characteristics you want in an Akita!

Good breeders only breed healthy dogs. Even before the breeding process, they will take their dogs to the vet to ensure they will produce healthy litters. Veterinarians will check the dog's general health and for common genetic diseases, like hip dysplasia, before issuing a health certificate to prove there are no known health concerns in each dog. Upon your request, your breeder should be eager to show their dogs' passed health standards.

After the puppies are born and before they are weaned, the breeder will take the litter to the vet to have them looked over. Oftentimes, young pups end up with worms, so a deworming treatment is standard puppy care. Also, at the same time, the hind dewclaws might be removed. During this first visit, the vet may be able to spot potential problems with a pup, which would prevent a responsible breeder from selling an unhealthy dog.

Photo Courtesy of Marshall Wolff

Your breeder should also give you information on their dogs' successes in the show ring and be able to prove their dogs come from champion stock, especially if you are interested in entering your new Akita into sanctioned events in the future. Any awards and accolades your breeder can show you will help verify the pup's good stock.

You also should talk to your breeder about the Akita or dog organizations in which they participate. A breeder who shows their caring and their commitment to their dogs in this way is someone who knows the breed and can answer all of your questions about your pup.

Finally, some breeders have guarantees to protect both parties if conflict arises over the puppy's health as he grows. These contracts vary from breeder to breeder; however, you should receive some sort of certificate of sale, information about kennel club organization registration, and a health certificate from the breeder's veterinarian.

The breeder might also ask the client to take their new pup to the vet for a second visit within the first few months of ownership; this is to verify the dog is indeed healthy. By doing this, the client makes sure they are getting what they paid for, and the breeder is protected from a client asking for a return on the basis of the pup's health. This type of guarantee protects the breeder's business if a client later returns the puppy for health reasons, but in reality, they simply cannot care for their Akita, and they demand a refund.

The guarantee might also stipulate the new owner cannot use the puppy for breeding purposes with other dogs, and it might require the pup to be spayed or neutered. This provision ensures the new owner cannot take business from the original breeder by using their stock. This may sound like extra work for the breeder and client, but these types of guarantees will make you feel more confident in knowing you are paying for a well-bred Akita. It also allows the breeder to feel comfortable about releasing their beloved pups.

Choosing the Perfect Pup

"I recommend letting the breeder or rescue choose the Akita that is right for you and your family. They have been with the dogs and know if their dominant or submissive, and which will fit in your family dynamic best."

CAROL FRIEDMAN
Sovereign Akitas

Once you have chosen a breeder, it is time to pick your perfect pup! Nowadays, this process often happens by photos on social media sites, but you cannot "feel" a dog's personality without meeting them in person! So, talk to your breeder and find a time when you can visit their home. Try to contact the breeder as soon as you possible; if a lot of people are looking for Akita puppies, they may be spoken for quickly.

When visiting and getting to know the puppies, sit in a room with them and let them come to you. This will allow you to get an idea of which puppies are outgoing and which ones are more reserved. Play with them for a while and note their personalities. Are they friendly? Do they play well with others? Do they seem curious? Needy? You may find the dogs with the best temperament are the ones that do not display any extreme behaviors. So, your ideal dog is probably not the most dominant or the most submissive of the group; nor are they the most attention-seeking or the shyest of the group. Breeders know puppies well, so they may match you with a pup that is perfect for you. If you tell your breeder what you are looking for in an Akita, they may be able to suggest the right puppy for the traits you desire and to sell you a puppy that best matches your personality.

Once you have chosen your puppy, your breeder will likely ask for a deposit on the pup, which is simply to protect the breeder from losing money if a potential client changes their mind at the last minute.

Do your research to make sure your breeder has the knowledge and experience needed to produce healthy litters that conform to AKC standards. The vetting process should not be rushed! The last thing you want to do when picking out a pup is to give business to an inexperienced or dishonest breeder who will sell you a sick puppy. Once you feel comfortable with your choice, all you need to do is wait until he is ready to come home with you!

CHAPTER 3
Preparing Your Home for Your Akita

While you are waiting for your puppy to be old enough to leave his mother, use the time to start preparing your home for your new dog. It is best to make preparations for your dog before your dog arrives because once he does, you will be very busy caring for your new Akita! You will find it is less stressful if your home and your family are ready for your new dog before he places his paws across your threshold! This chapter will guide you through the preparations you must make before your dog settles in.

Photo Courtesy of Samantha Mellors

The Protective Akita

"Akitas need to be an important member of the family. They don't require as much exercise as a person would think. They are loving and protective, and make great family pets if trained right and trained young."

VICKY ALLEN
Allens Akitas

One of the defining qualities of the Akita is that he is a protector. This means your dog might be slow to warm up to strangers or other dogs once he arrives. This does not mean your dog will be aggressive toward others, but he may be naturally wary of unfamiliar people and animals. Because of this, it is important to set realistic expectations for your Akita.

You cannot expect him to be best friends with your young children or other pets without lots of socialization. Also, you cannot expect your Akita to be the center of attention every time you entertain visitors. Forcing your Akita to be social in every new situation may lead to unwanted behaviors later on. Much of your preparation in the early days should address making him feel comfortable and secure in his new home.

Preparing Your Family and Your Pets

Before you bring your Akita home, talk to the people in your family about the proper way to behave around a dog. This message is especially important for young children, as they may not have much experience with dogs, and they may not understand that dogs are animals and need to be treated as such. Tell the children in your household they need to be calm and kind to the Akita puppy. Remind them that dogs do not like to be grabbed or cornered, and they need their own space – just like people. Akitas like to play, but they may confuse play with danger if the play is too rough or the children are loud or make sudden movements. Of course, no dog should be left with children without proper adult supervision. If handled properly, your children and your new Akita puppy will get along just fine!

The adults in your household may also need to be reminded about how to interact with a dog. Never be too quick to approach a dog and do not force an Akita to spend time with you if he acts hesitant. It is better to let an Akita approach you when he is ready instead of forcing yourself on him. Holding out a hand or an arm to sniff first and offering a treat can help an Akita feel more comfortable around strangers.

Pets can be more difficult than family to prepare for your new Akita because they cannot be lectured on how to behave around a new dog! If your animals are not used to being around dogs, this might be an appropriate time to take your pets to the dog park to interact with other animals or to introduce your cat (or other pets) to a friend's dog. This will prevent them

Photo Courtesy
of Sophie Emma Windham

from being completely caught off guard by a strange canine that walks through your front door! However, this is a process that might need quite a bit of work. There is only so much socialization you can accomplish in a few weeks, especially if your current pets are adults!

Make sure every animal in your home has its own space. If you have a cat, build a cat tree or platform that only your cat can reach if she needs to escape contact with your dog. Or use a baby gate in a spare room that will allow your cat to get the space she needs. If you own another dog, give him his own crate that he can enter when he is overwhelmed by a new puppy or use gates to section off parts of your home so each animal gets some alone time if he needs it. Later chapters will discuss how to socialize your pets once you bring your new Akita home.

CELEBRITY DOGS
Victory Dog

Alina Zagitova, a Russian champion figure skater, received an Akita puppy from a group that works to preserve the breed in 2018. She named the puppy Masaru, which means "victory" in Japanese. Zagitova fell in love with the Akita breed while she was in Japan preparing for the Pyeongchang Winter Olympics and asked her mom to buy her a puppy if she did well at the Olympics.

Preparing Your Home

Preparing your home for a new puppy is much like baby-proofing a home for a newborn. Puppies are curious creatures who explore the world through tasting, chewing, and digging. At this stage in their life, they do not understand rules about living in a human's house - they simply follow their puppy instinct! Due to the nature of the beast, you must dog-proof your home in order to prevent the destruction of property and to keep your new pup safe in a world he does not yet quite understand.

To start, look around your house at a dog's level. What could your dog possibly reach while exploring your home? Anything kept on the floor will likely be chewed or eaten by a puppy. For instance, if your habit is to fling dirty clothes on your bedroom floor when you change, your Akita may swallow a sock. If you leave your shoes by the door, your Akita may chew on them because it feels good on their teething mouth. Loose cords around your entertainment system are unfamiliar, so an Akita may give them a nibble to see what they are. Even your table legs and baseboards are not off-limits to a dog that may be bored, curious, or anxious.

As a general rule, if something is within your Akita's reach, you can expect it to be chewed on. This can be dangerous and destructive so put anything low to the ground in cupboards, drawers, or higher shelves and change any of your own messy habits before bringing your dog home!

Also, remember your puppy will have limited control over his bladder and bowels for several months. If you have a lot of carpeting in your home, you may want to keep those places off-limits to your Akita pup or to place protective coverings on the floor. Many puppy owners set up baby gates or a play pen on hard floors, then cover those floors in newspaper or potty pads in order to protect surfaces. More information about housetraining will be addressed in a later chapter, but it is a good idea to think about how you will keep your floors sanitary with a new pup in your home.

Not sure where to start with puppy-proofing your home? You can use the following checklist to cover the basics until you know what your Akita is interested in exploring:

- Keep shoes in a closet, instead of by the door
- Move cleaning supplies and other toxic chemicals to a secure location, such as a high shelf in a closet or garage
- If you keep books, remote controls, or any other item on a low coffee table or end table, move them to a spot where your Akita cannot reach
- Secure loose cords around electronics and hide them behind sturdy furniture
- Close toilet lids or close bathroom doors to keep a puppy from drinking out of the toilet or digging through the trash
- Use trashcans with dog-proof lids
- Store all food in the refrigerator, pantry, or cupboard; avoid leaving food on the counter or table
- Put laundry in a tall basket so your dog cannot steal or eat your clothes
- Put anything at dog-level out of reach until your Akita outgrows the puppy stage
- Use baby gates to close off areas you do not want a puppy to explore while unattended

Of course, preparing your home for a dog is more than just keeping your belongings safe. During this prep time, you will want to find ways to make your Akita feel at home. Choose a spot where you spend a lot of time and give your Akita an area where he can have his own space yet still be close to you. For instance, if you love to watch movies in your living room, put a dog bed or crate in a corner of the room. This way, your dog can feel safe in his "den" and still feel close to you. A comfy bed or a blanket-lined crate can make your dog feel cozy and safe wherever you spend time together. Keep a few dog toys and chews close by, and your pup will be happy in his new home!

Photo Courtesy of Samantha Mastrolia

Getting Your Yard Ready for Your Akita

If you have a backyard, you will want to make sure it is dog-proofed and safe for your new Akita, just like you did with your house. Dogs love to spend time in the fresh air and can find tons of enjoyment by sniffing everything they can find! However, you will want to make sure your dog is safe in your yard and can be left there unattended for short periods of time.

The first thing you must realize...Akitas can be escape artists! This means you will need a sturdy fence around your yard to keep your new dog from wandering off. You will want your fence to be constructed in a way that it is partially buried or is very low to the ground. If not, and your Akira feels like escaping, it will not take him long to dig a hole under your fence. A tall privacy fence is great for containing this breed of dog. Not only will it keep your dog from escaping your yard, but it will also keep your Akita from seeing strange people and dogs on the outside, which will reduce his protective instinct. Short, chain-link fences are a less expensive alternative to a tall privacy fence, but anything too short may allow your adult Akita to jump over the top. Plus, a see-through fence of this nature will make it easy for your dog to see everyone who is coming and going...and that will drive your alert and protective Akita crazy!

Some dog owners use invisible fences if they cannot build a privacy or chain-link fence or if their yard is too large for these types of structures. An invisible fence works on the premise it will deliver a shock to your dog, through his collar, if he goes beyond the fence line. Eventually, your dog will learn the perimeter of your yard and will stay within its boundaries.

However, keep in mind there is no physical barrier keeping your dog contained, and some dogs become so interested in chasing something outside of their invisible fence they overpower the shock and escape anyway. Unable to get back into the yard without being shocked again, your dog might not know what to do from there.

You also have to remember, with no physical barrier, any person or animal can walk into your yard, which might antagonize your dog or result in injury for all parties involved. In most situations, this type of fence can be highly effective with a majority of dogs, but a traditional fence will give you more peace of mind knowing your dog will not be able to run off if he is momentarily unattended.

Next, make sure there are no dangerous chemicals in the yard that are within your Akita's reach. Pesticides, herbicides, and other poisons can be fatal to dogs if ingested. These products should be kept in a closed shed or garage where a dog cannot get into them.

You may even reconsider which products you use around your home. For instance, certain types of rodent killers are only effective if left out until the problem is eliminated. If a dog wanders around the yard or garage and finds bait or poison meant for another animal, he may try to eat it. So, if you are dealing with animals burrowing in your yard, you might need to find a non-toxic alternative or repellant. Also, pay close attention to the directions for the yard products you use. The labels will instruct you how to use the product in a way that does its job but also keeps pets safe. Always use an abundance of caution, for your Akita's sake, when caring for your yard.

Finally, you will also want to think carefully about the plants in your landscaping. Some plants are toxic to dogs and can be fatal if ingested in substantial amounts. For example, different types of lilies, ivy, flower bulbs, and rhubarb leaves are all common outdoor plants that can make a dog extremely sick. This does not necessarily mean you need to tear out all existing plants around your home! Yet, keep in mind the type of flowers and shrubbery currently in your gardens and landscaping. Always deter your dog from eating decorative plants, both inside and outside, and keep an eye on your dog at all times. If he appears to take interest in tasting a plant, clap your hands, give him a firm "No," and redirect his attention. When you plant new flowers and shrubs in the future, consider planting things that are safe for dogs.

Necessary Supplies for Your Akita

"Get lots of chew toys. Your Akita puppy will need them for when they're cutting and losing their teeth. Otherwise, they will eat you furniture."

VICKY ALLEN
Allens Akitas

Whether you currently own a dog or if this is your first canine, you will need to gather supplies before the day of arrival. The process of purchasing supplies can seem overwhelming and expensive, but many of the items you purchase will last for many years, if not your dog's entire lifetime. High-quality pet products may cost more upfront, but they will save you money in the long run. While it is not necessary to buy all of your dog's supplies before you bring him home, it is helpful to have a majority of the supplies on hand, so you do not have to worry about shopping trips in between caring for your new puppy.

Photo Courtesy
of Róbert Foki

This checklist is not a comprehensive list of everything your dog may need, but it can be used as a starting point to prevent overlooking any of the essentials.

- Flat collar and sturdy four to six foot leash
- Identification tag
- Food and water dishes (ceramic or stainless-steel work well)
- Puppy food and training treats
- Pin brush and slicker brush
- Nail clippers or grinders
- Bed
- Crate
- Size-appropriate chew toys
- Tug toys, balls, and stuffed animals
- Puppy pads
- Towels
- Enzymatic cleaner for potty messes
- Gates or playpen

Preparing before your new dog's arrival will reduce stress and free up more time for you to play with and to train your dog. Your goal is to make your home a safe and comfortable place for your Akita, as well as your family members and other pets. The more work you put into your preparation, the smoother the transition will be. Once you have prepared your family, your house, and your yard for your new Akita, it is time to bring him home!

CHAPTER 4
Bringing Your Akita Home

F inally, the day arrives to bring home your new Akita! After doing so much research, planning, and preparing, it is time to enjoy your new puppy. The first few days will be a big transition for both you and your new pup, so this chapter will guide you through a couple more milestones of your new life with your Akita.

Photo Courtesy of Louisa Vanhoutte

The Importance of Having a Plan

Puppies require a lot of attention...this is a fact! In order to help them acclimate to your home and to teach them the rules, you have to constantly supervise them so you can correct unwanted behaviors right from the start. Not only will puppies want to play with you throughout the day, but they will also need frequent bathroom breaks!

Remember, the early days in your home will also be stressful for a new puppy. He will be away from his mother and siblings for the first time in his life. He will leave the only home he has ever known to live in a new place with different sights, sounds, and smells. Akitas are sensitive dogs that feed off their owner's emotions, so if you are stressed with caring for your new puppy, your puppy will feel your anxiety! Planning ahead of time will not eliminate all stress for you or your new pup, but it will make the early days much more enjoyable!

The Ride Home

Your puppy is understandably going to be nervous when you bring him home. These nerves might even turn into unpleasant feelings about being in a car in general, which can make car travel difficult in the future. In order to have a smooth transition from breeder or animal shelter to home, you will want to keep your dog calm and comforted on the ride home.

If possible, your best option is to have a family member or friend accompany you on this journey. A dog can be a distraction to a driver as it is, but a new puppy can be very needy. It will be a much less stressful ride – for everyone - if you sit beside your puppy in his crate as your friend drives the car. I guarantee your pup will feel more at ease with you by his side assuring him everything will be alright! You may even want to bring a few training treats to reward him for staying calm as you travel.

If you cannot bring someone on this trip to help with the pickup, be sure to have a small crate or dog carrier with you to secure in the back seat. Dogs should always be restrained while traveling in case of an accident. It is also unsafe to drive with a puppy on your lap or to have a puppy wandering around your car as you drive. This will be covered in detail in a later chapter.

For this first trip home, you will also want to put a seat protector or old towels on the car seat in case your pup is sick or has an accident.

The First Night Home

"Be patient with them. Their world has changed 100% from living with their mother, siblings and breeder. They are very intelligent and will be able to adapt to their new surroundings and routine, but it can take a little time."

LINDA BACCO
Shogitai Akitas

Photo Courtesy
of Brad and Allison Madsen

Photo Courtesy of Tara Everett

Once you are settled in, your puppy will get so much play time during the day he will probably be too exhausted and happy to become lonely or to cry. However, the nighttime might be a different story. While you try to sleep, your dog will be lonely without your constant attention, and he will want to go outside to potty. While it is likely your dog will not sleep through the night for the first few weeks, there are some things you can do to make bedtime easier on everyone.

First, make sure your dog's exercise needs are met every day. A tired dog is a good dog, and your dog is less likely to get into trouble if he is tired out from his daily routine. Early in the evening, take your pup on a walk or run around your backyard in hopes of tiring him out. Also, make sure the last thing you do before going to bed is let your dog outside to go to the bathroom one last time. This should prevent him from needing to go for several hours.

Photo Courtesy
of T&J Jennings
@Makana_Bear and @Panzie_Bear on IG

You might also want to restrict food and water access to some degree prior to bedtime, so his little bladder is relatively empty at the beginning of the night. (However, it is not a good idea to prevent access to water for prolonged periods of time, as your dog will need to stay hydrated.)

You will also want to consider where your dog sleeps. Many owners do not allow their dog to sleep on the bed. If you do not want your big, adult Akita to share your bed, do not allow your cute, cuddly Akita puppy to share your bed! It can be extremely hard to teach your dog to sleep on the floor if he is accustomed to sleeping on your bed. However, if your puppy's bed is too far away from you, this might cause him to cry more because he will feel lonely. The decision where your Akita should sleep can be a delicate balance!

If your puppy cries and hates being away from you during the night, try placing his crate in your bedroom with the front of the crate facing your bed. He will be able to see, smell, and hear you, but he will not be climbing all over you while you are trying to sleep! Plus, when he cries to go to the bathroom, you will be able to hear him and take him outside immediately.

When you take the puppy out during the middle of the night, do not pet him or play with him; he needs to learn this is not playtime - this is business! If you are too friendly during these midnight outings, he will get the wrong message, so once your puppy does his business and returns to his crate, close the gate behind him and go back to bed.

Especially in the early days, you will probably have to take your puppy outside a couple times during the middle of the night, but eventually he will be able to sleep through the night. Do not despair!

Keeping Your Akita Comfortable at the Vet

You and your puppy should visit the vet soon after bringing your dog home. Puppies receive their first shots, known as booster shots, within a short timeframe after birth. During this time, your veterinarian will perform a short examination to make sure your pup is healthy and is developing normally.

Unfortunately, many dogs have a fear of going to the vet. After all, it is a strange place with unusual smells, unfamiliar animals in the waiting room, and a stranger that pokes and prods him for no apparent reason! At times, dogs will have to experience uncomfortable sensations, like shots, blood draws, or ear cleanings. Without positive reinforcement, these negative feelings associated with the vet can turn into fear and resistance during future visits.

First, you will need to choose a veterinarian with whom you are comfortable. If you do not have a regular vet, talk to friends or people in your community about their favorite animal clinic. A good place to start is always with a recommendation from someone whose opinion you trust. If your breeder is local, they will probably love to give you a recommendation, which will also be reassuring to know the vet is already familiar with the Akita breed of dog.

You should also consider the services each clinic offers its patients. Some clinics have a full range of services and

FUN FACT
Akita Museum

Located in Odate, Japan is a museum dedicated to the Akita breed. The museum was founded by the Akita Dog Preservation Society and inspired by an Akita named Hashiko who gained international fame for his loyalty.

Photo Courtesy of Charlotte Arcand

perform surgeries, take x-rays and scans, analyze samples in an in-house lab, and provide emergency care. Generally, smaller clinics do not have the means to provide all of these services, but can refer a patient to a larger clinic, if needed.

One way to prepare your pup for the vet is to practice some of the experiences he will go through during a veterinarian visit...this starts with the drive. By going on short drives with your pup and by giving him treats if he remains calm, you will build positive connections with simply riding in the car.

Also, begin organizing interactions with adults with whom your dog is unfamiliar. This should make your dog feel more comfortable around people he does not know - like the vet. Ask a few trusted friends to meet your dog and to give him a treat or two, so your dog realizes most people he meets are not there to do him harm.

Once you are at the vet's office, use a calm and soothing voice when talking to your dog in hopes of keeping him calm, too. If you find yourself becoming nervous over your puppy getting poked and prodded by the vet, try to remain in control of your emotions...for your dog's sake. Your dog will definitely pick up on your nervous feelings, which will also manifest in your Akita's reaction to the situation. If you act as though everything is normal, your dog will be more likely to stay calm and relaxed, too.

Finally, give your dog tons of praise during and after the appointment with the veterinarian. Celebrate a positive trip to the vet by going on a walk or playing with a favorite toy once you leave the office. Let your dog know he did an excellent job at the vet's visit...he may even get excited to go to the vet in the future!

A later chapter will give more details about the differences between veterinary clinics.

Cost Breakdown for the First Year

Part of dog ownership includes budgeting for your puppy's needs throughout his life. Many expenses are one-time expenses; for example, purchasing your puppy or buying food dishes and brushes. Other expenses happen regularly and can be easily budgeted for, such as food, preventative medications, and yearly checkups. Then, there are some expenses - emergency veterinarian care or surgery - that can be completely unexpected. Becoming a dog owner can be expensive, and you do not want to be put in a situation where you may forgo necessary supplies or care for your Akita because you cannot afford it.

*Photo Courtesy
of Nathanael Wilson*

The chart below will give you a general overview of how much dog care costs in the first year of ownership, so you will be better prepared to create your own dog budget.

Adoption	$100 - $250
Buying a Puppy	$700 - $1,500+
Veterinarian Care	$135 - $550+
Dental Care	$0 - $250
Basic Supplies	$50 - $250
Food	$300 - $750+
Toys and Treats	$50 - $250
Crates	$60 - $400+
Training	$100 - $2000

The above figures may seem pretty high, but the healthiness and happiness of your Akita is well worth the expense. Plus, if you start preparing for these expenses before you bring your dog home, you may be able to find good deals on some everyday supplies.

CHAPTER 5
Being a Puppy Parent

"As with any working class dog the Akita needs someone to be the pack leader. The Akita loves their family and children but needs to be respected."

CAROL FRIEDMAN
Sovereign Akitas

Life with a new puppy can be loads of fun...especially an Akita puppy! This breed of puppy is adorable and cuddly, has tons of playful energy, and will be your protector for the rest of their lives. Nonetheless, being the owner of a new puppy is one big responsibility! Not only will your pup constantly keep you on your toes, but the way you interact with your puppy in the first few months of ownership will form his personality, his daily

Photo Courtesy of Vivi Angeru

routine, and his experience with others. Hard work in these early months will prepare your Akita for a successful life as your new-found friend!

On the other hand, not working consistently with your dog during his formative years will make his life unorganized and with no structure, which will also make it tougher to train him as an adult. This chapter will help you understand why your puppy behaves the way he does, and it will give you tips on how to help him adjust to life as a member of your household.

Setting Realistic Expectations

Raising a puppy can be frustrating if you are unprepared for the needs of your new puppy. Perhaps you have gotten used to taking care of an adult dog; starting over with an Akita puppy takes much more time and energy plus many different skills. It is important to understand what your young Akita can and cannot do right from the beginning.

At this point in your Akita's life, your dog has never been away from his mother or siblings, and he probably has limited experience being in someone's home. A puppy will not automatically know he is not supposed to potty in the house or that playtime during the middle of the night is not allowed. You should also not feel disheartened if you have tried to teach your puppy these basic skills, and he has been slow to understand your commands. Young puppies lack the mental maturity to comprehend what you are asking them to do. It is good to practice pre-training skills with your pup, but do not expect him to be ready for the showring at five months old! Dogs will ultimately learn how to behave in a human household after being taught certain rules...over an extended period of time.

AKITA IN FILM
Hachiko

Hachiko the Akita is so famous for his loyalty that not only is he the subject of two films, but there are at least two known statues of him. Hachiko was owned by Eizaburo Ueno, a professor at Tokyo University in Japan. The loyal dog accompanied Eizaburo to the train station every day for his commute to work. One day, Eizaburo didn't return, as he had passed away suddenly from a cerebral hemorrhage at work. Though Hachiko moved in with a new family, he still returned to the Shibuya Train Station every morning to wait for his late owner. When a Japanese newspaper picked up the story in 1932, Hachiko gained celebrity status across Japan. In 1934, a statue of Hachiko was unveiled at the Shibuya Train Station, which remains a popular attraction to this day. There are also several films featuring Hachiko's story.

Photo Courtesy
of Elfi Bonn

For example, a puppy has little concept of a piece of furniture, let alone the understanding needed to know why he should not be chewing on a chair's wooden leg! Your puppy is not "bad" if he causes a little chaos or a small mess in your home – that is just part of being a puppy! During this time, correct the problems that you can, avoid as many potential problems as possible, and give yourself (and your puppy) some space to learn how to work together.

If you have other people living in your household, it is good to have a conversation explaining how you will raise your Akita. People have many different ideas about how to raise a dog, often learned from watching a parent or friend care for a family pet. While it can be useful to consider different experiences and ideas regarding dog care, consistency is key.

If you want to housetrain your puppy by only allowing him to go to the bathroom outside, but your partner directs your pup to a potty pad inside... your puppy will learn contradicting rules that will cause confusion and hamper your training efforts.

Perhaps your roommate came from a household where pets were not allowed to sit on furniture, but you plan on snuggling on the couch with your Akita every chance you get! Together, you will have to decide on household rules for your new puppy, or your Akita will be confused by conflicting messages and that will cause problems for everyone concerned. Over time, puppies do learn how to live with a new family in a new home but not without consistent practice and training.

Common Puppy Problems

In the beginning, you might notice that your puppy can be naughty and seems to get into trouble whenever you turn your back! This is perfectly normal, as our expectations for how our dog should act do not always align with how a puppy wants to behave. However, there are several easy fixes to common problems when first training your puppy.

First, keep in mind the best way for your puppy to learn any new behavior is through repetition. He will not learn he should use the outside as his bathroom after the very first try. However, with enough repetition, redirection, and positive reinforcement, your puppy will behave the way you want him to behave. Here are a few common issues dog owners frequently work through during the first year of their dog's life:

Photo Courtesy
of Meaha Everson-Dunkley

Biting

Puppies do not bite because they are aggressive, or they want to hurt someone. Much like people use their hands to manipulate things, dogs use their mouths to explore the world around them. Your puppy will chew on objects (or people) because he wants to understand and learn about his surroundings. Puppies will also bite fingers and toes because that is how puppies play with one another. It might be painful when a dog nibbles on your fingers because puppy teeth are very sharp; it does not mean he is a vicious dog. He just has not learned that his bite can hurt others!

This behavior has a fairly simple fix. When puppies play with one another and one receives a painful bite, you will hear a high-pitched yelping sound from the injured pup. This signals to the other puppy he has caused his play-mate pain, which will teach him to be gentle the next time the two puppies play together. If your puppy playfully nips you, signal to him his actions are not allowed by saying, "Ouch!" in a high-pitched voice mimicking the puppy yelp. If you do this every time your puppy bites you, he will learn to stop. Then, offer him a chewing alternative, such as a bone or rawhide toy, which will signal biting can be okay but only with certain objects - definitely not people!

Chewing

As mentioned earlier, sometimes your puppy may chew on your belong-ings because he is exploring his new surroundings, but he may also be chewing on solid objects because he is teething, bored, or anxious.

The teething process can cause irritation in your puppy's mouth, so chewing can help push the adult teeth through the gums and soothe the pain. Dogs also chew objects for their own entertainment or as a stress reliever. If your dog does not have a bone or toy to play with or to chew, he will gnaw on anything he can find - furniture, shoes, and other common household items. Because you cannot - and should not - prevent your dog from chewing all objects, it is important to keep your personal and house-hold items out of the puppy's reach and to keep plenty of dog-safe chew toys available for him. As your Akita grows, you will want to swap out the pup-py-sized chew toys for larger ones, so your dog does not choke on smaller toys or on pieces he has bitten off the original plaything.

Accidents

Having an "accident" in the house is a common problem for new puppy parents. While dogs generally do not soil their living areas (which is helpful when crate training your dog), they lack the understanding to know their waste is a problem in your home. When housetraining your dog, repetition and positive reinforcement are the key to success. With enough redirection and positive feedback, he will eventually understand he is only supposed to go to the bathroom when he is outside. Steps in housetraining your puppy will be covered in detail in the next chapter.

Jumping Up

There is no doubt puppies are curious creatures who love to explore their surroundings! Naturally, your dog may show his excitement over an unfamiliar visitor by greeting them and by jumping up on them. When puppies jump at a person, it is cute...when big adult dogs jump up, it can be very scary and threatening, or it can cause injuries to everyone involved. If you do not want your Akita to jump on people as an adult dog, correct this behavior as a puppy!

Dogs that jump up on people usually do this out of excitement or because they want immediate attention; they know people will pet them if they are within reach. To break this bad habit, remove the attention the dog is seeking. When your dog starts to jump up on you, turn your back to him. When all four paws are back on the ground, reward him for not jumping.

Photo Courtesy of Róbert Foki

Separation Anxiety

As mentioned previously, Akitas are sensitive dogs who want nothing more than to spend lots of time with their owner. When they are left alone, this trait leaves them susceptible to separation anxiety. Separation anxiety refers to the feelings and associated behaviors a dog will display when he is "separated" from his owner. Reasons a dog might display separation anxiety may be due to behavioral problems or to illnesses related to elevated stress levels. Excessive crying or barking, scratching, chewing, and having accidents in the house or their crate are all symptoms of an anxiety problem. If you return home from an outing and your dog has caused destruction in your home, it might be because your absence was so distressing that he needed an outlet for his pent-up energy and anxiety. Luckily, there are some things you can do to reduce this anxiety.

*Photo Courtesy
of Adriana Balas*

First, make sure your dog's needs are met before you leave home. Lots of play, a brisk walk, and a trip outside to go to the bathroom will cover some of your dog's physical needs, so he doesn't have as much nervous energy when you are away. Make sure there are plenty of toys and chew toys readily available to keep your puppy occupied. You might fill a puzzle toy with his favorite snack, which can keep your dog entertained immediately after you leave the house and for some time after.

A dog crate can also keep your dog safe, comfortable, and calm while you are away. Many dogs enjoy being in crates for short periods of time because it mimics the feeling of being in a den. Also, if your dog is comfortable being contained in a crate, it means that he cannot be destructive while you are away. If you are not using a crate, consider putting up a baby gate so your dog cannot wander around your home looking for things to do! (Later chapters will discuss crate training in more detail.)

You also should consider the message you are sending your dog when you leave the house and when you return. Too much excitement when leaving or returning home can signal to a dog that your absence is a big deal. This, in turn, can build up your dog's feelings of anxiety at the mere idea of you leaving the house.

If you feel your dog is prone to separation anxiety, leave your home without drawing attention to your actions and return in the same manner. If your comings and goings are a normal part of every day, your dog will realize it is a regular part of his routine, and he will be a much happier dog in the long run!

If you have tried everything and your dog still suffers from anxiety when he is left alone, arrange for someone else to spend time with him. Your dog may respond well to having a dog walker visit during the day, or your dog may enjoy playing at a doggy daycare until you return. An Akita is not a good breed for an owner who spends a lot of time away from home. If you cannot spend a lot of time with this dog, consider a different breed or make arrangements for someone to keep your dog company.

Finally, if nothing you try seems to help, talk to your veterinarian about medically treating your dog's separation anxiety. Your vet might recommend an over-the-counter herbal supplement, or they may prescribe medication. Pharmaceuticals are often used as a last resort for separation anxiety, so always work on treating the behavioral symptoms before turning to medication.

CHAPTER 6
Potty Training

"Akita puppies are very easily housetrained. My puppies have been going out to potty since before they left for their new homes. Akitas don't like using the bathroom inside so be sure to take the puppy out every few hours."

CAROL FRIEDMAN
Sovereign Akitas

Potty training is perhaps the most important skill you will teach your Akita pup during the first few months of his life in his new home. While occasional accidents in the early months are to be expected, frequent pet messes can be detrimental to the cleanliness of your home and can become a health hazard. If your dog cannot reliably go to the bathroom outside, you will be limited in your ability to leave the house for longer than a few hours, and your Akita will not be welcome in other people's homes.

Photo Courtesy
of Tara Everett

It takes a lot of time and attention to housetrain your pup, but this chapter will guide you through the potty-training process and give you tips that will make training much easier.

Being Consistent

Consistency is key when it comes to dog training, and potty training is no exception. Your Akita will depend on you to take him outside whenever he needs to go, which is not always easy for a dog to communicate to their owner. Your dog may whine or paw at the door when he needs to go outside, but he may also whine for completely unrelated issues. Circling or looking for a place to squat is an immediate warning sign, but you will want to take your dog outside before he gets to this point.

To prevent accidents, take your dog outside on a regular schedule. Go outside the very first thing in the morning, every few hours throughout the day, and the last thing before bed. Going outside every hour (or even every half hour) may seem like overkill, but if your dog successfully uses the bathroom outside, you are building important skills.

When you take your pup outside, put him on a leash and guide him to the same spot in the yard every time. Dogs tend to use the perimeter of the yard to do their business because it is on the edge of their play space. Guide your dog to a corner of the yard, let him sniff around the spot for a minute, and give him a treat when he does his business. If he doesn't go after a few minutes, it might not be time yet. Guide your dog back inside and wait until he is ready. Thirty minutes later, take your dog to the same spot. After a successful trip, give him a reward.

Options for Potty Training

Due to the nature of a young puppy's bladder size, an accident inside is bound to happen at some point. Scrubbing pet stains out of your carpet is the last thing you want to do - it will happen – so be vigilant and be prepared.

Some puppy owners like to use disposable pee pads for the floor, which can be purchased at a pet store. They are placed on the floor as a place for your puppy to relieve himself and to protect the floor underneath. The potty pads are absorbent and contain a special scent that attracts your pup to use them. Over time, you can move the pad to the doorway, little by little, and then outside, in hopes your dog will move his business totally outside.

These potty pads can be used for puppies who are learning how to control their bodily functions or in situations where it is impossible to take a dog outside (for example, in inclement weather). The pads work better than newspaper as a floor covering because your dog will be attracted to them and will use it as a place to relieve himself. However, keep in mind if your dog becomes too accustomed to using potty pads, he may be resistant to moving this action outside. Also, the price of buying disposable products adds up over time, which may not be in your puppy-care budget. Puppy pads are useful during the early days and in special circumstances, but they are not an ideal, long-term solution for your Akita's bathroom needs.

Photo Courtesy
of T&J Jennings
@Makana_Bear and @Panzie_Bear on IG

Keeping it Positive

As with all facets of dog training, positivity is the best way to reinforce good behavior. Every time your dog uses the bathroom outside, you have created a teachable moment which can be positively reinforced. After a successful bathroom outing, give your Akita pup some sort of reward. Some dogs are crazy for treats while others feel loved when they get a little playtime as a reward. Akitas are people-pleasers, so praise is definitely necessary! A "good boy" and a few pats on the head will teach your Akita he did something exceptionally good, which will cause him to repeat the behavior in the future in hopes of getting the same prize.

If your dog has an accident inside the house, punishment is not an effective response, and it can negate any positive reinforcement you have shown him in the past.

When it appears your Akita might have an accident inside the house, you can get your dog's attention with simply a clap or a "Hey!" and then redirect him to go outside. If you cannot make it outside in time, it is fine to tell your dog, "No," so he knows he did not do what he was supposed to do; however, do not act out in anger.

Many people believe that owners should yell and rub a dog's nose in the accident, so they connect the smell with your anger. However, dog memories do not work the same way human memories do. You may be able to scold a young child for making a mess after the fact, but that is only because you and the child share a common language.

A dog can discern tone but does not understand the content behind your message. Therefore, when someone shouts at a dog because there is a stain on the carpet, the dog knows the owner is upset, but he does not necessarily understand why. He might realize the anger is in response to the accident, but this might also lead to the dog hiding their mess in the future in hopes of avoiding another angry response.

When a dog has an accident that you did not witness, you have lost a teachable moment. When you find yourself in this situation, do not scold your dog, but thoroughly clean up the mess so he does not try to use that spot as a bathroom again. An enzymatic cleaner made specifically for pet messes works better than soap and water because it breaks down the scents that attract dogs to a bathroom spot. This should prevent your dog (or other dogs) from using the same spot simply because they can detect a urine smell.

Potty Training an Adult Akita

Sometimes, adult dogs also have accidents in the house. This could be because they were not trained as a puppy, they experienced trauma that resulted in behavioral issues, or they have health issues that cause incontinence. If your adult Akita is not potty trained and is in good health, you can easily re-train an adult dog to go to the bathroom outside. This will take lots of positive reinforcement because your Akita may need to shed

Photo Courtesy of Chris Fowkes

negative feelings towards potty training and to replace them with positive associations.

If your dog has other fears, you might need to address these anxieties before successfully housetraining your adult dog. For example, if your Akita is severely distrustful of others, try taking him to use the bathroom in a place where he does not have to see or hear other people. Or, if your Akita was previously punished whenever he had an accident, make sure you hide any frustration when cleaning up the mess.

As with potty training puppies, lots of practice and positive reinforcement are key. Even after your Akita has mastered potty training, it does not hurt to praise your dog every time he is successful. If you are unable to potty train your adult Akita, you may want to visit the vet or ask a behavioral specialist for help. Your dog's issues with potty training might be physical, or they might simply require an expert for behavior modification in order to get this habit under control.

Crates, Playpens, and Doggy Doors

Since it can be hard to keep an eye on a puppy at all times, you will want to contain your puppy to one spot in the house for those times when you simply cannot watch him. This is where crate training can be especially useful – now and throughout your dog's life.

This method of protection can also allow your dog to safely travel on drives in the car or on airplanes. You might use the crate to drive to the vet or the dog boarder, or your Akita might use it in your home as his safe space when he is feeling overwhelmed.

Crates are also useful when it comes to potty training because dogs generally avoid going to the bathroom in the area where they live – their "den." This means if you keep your puppy in his crate for short periods of time when you cannot watch him, this should act as an incentive to "hold it" until you let him outside.

To train a puppy to go into their crate, place food, water, treats, or toys inside the enclosure. Do not coax or push your dog inside the crate; instead, let him enter on his own. Give him praise when he goes inside to investigate. Slowly build up his time spent in the crate until you can close the door with your dog inside, and you can leave the room without your dog panicking.

Your dog should eventually feel safe and secure inside his crate, which makes it a useful spot to hang out during a thunderstorm or other frightening moments. Additionally, a crate can be a good "chill out" spot for your Akita if he becomes overwhelmed or irritated with other pets, children, or houseguests.

When traveling, a crate can keep your dog restrained in the car, while the rigid walls of the container can also protect him from debris in the event of an accident. As you can see, there are a lot of benefits to crate training your dog!

If crate training does not appeal to your Akita - some dogs simply do not like to go into small spaces - setting up a playpen or a gate can keep your puppy from roaming all over the house and possibly leaving messes every-where. Placing your puppy in a playpen in the kitchen, or in other centrally located rooms with hard floors that are easy to clean, works very well. Since your Akita will want to spend as much time as possible being close to you, you would not set up his play space in a room that is often vacant; keep him close to the action!

Photo Courtesy of Celia Facenda

If you want to give your dog more room to roam than in a playpen, baby gates are useful for blocking off rooms that are off-limits to your puppy, such as a living room with new couches or a carpeted bedroom. These gates work well because your dog feels he has room to explore, but you are controlling where he goes and what he does!

Playpens and gates are also great for new dog owners because they are easy to store once your adult Akita no longer needs the barriers.

Doggy doors are another method of giving your dog more freedom when it comes to moving around the house and to making independent bathroom trips outside. These small "trap doors" can be purchased at a pet store or a home improvement store and should be installed in your existing doors. When your dog feels the urge to go to the bathroom, he will not need to rely on you to take him outside; instead, he can push through the doggy dog, do his business outside, and return to the house.

These doors work well if you have a secure fence in your yard or if you are unable to let your dog out as often as he needs. It is also useful for the Akita that loves to be outside for the majority of the day. If you work away from home, you can feel at ease knowing your dog can explore the backyard during the day with the opportunity to come inside if the weather changes.

To train your dog how to use a doggy door, have him stand on one side of the door and place a valued treat on the other side. Keep the flap open so he can see the treat, and so he can go through the door to the outdoors. Once he can walk through the hole, lower the door flap and repeat the process until he feels comfortable walking through without the use of treats. Avoid forcing your dog through the doggy door because this may cause a negative association that might prevent him from using the door in the future.

You need to realize there are some downsides to installing a doggy door in your home – things you need to consider before the installation. A doggy door is a permanent change to the construction of your home, and it will make your home more susceptible to the outdoors. Not only will it let cold or hot air inside, but there is the potential for a small animal to enter your home along with your dog. Also, if your Akita is an accomplished backyard hunter, he may even bring his prizes inside to show you! So...before installing a doggy door, decide if the positives outweigh the potential negatives.

Potty training can be a positive experience for you and your Akita puppy if you remember to keep the training fun! Give your dog tons of praise when he accomplishes his goal and avoid punishment and fear-based tactics at all costs. Be vigilant with your schedule, so you avoid as many accidents in the house as possible and so you increase your chances for reinforceable behaviors. Stay positive, and before long, your puppy will be able to communicate his needs to you so he can do his business outside and avoid leaving a mess inside.

CHAPTER 7
Socializing with People and Animals

"Puppy Kindergarten is a must! I find the window of dog tolerance closes around 12-16 weeks. Allowing them play sessions during a group training class gives a positive experience around other dogs."

LINDA BACCO
Shogitai Akitas

Photo Courtesy of James & Victoria Robison

Socialization is an under-rated and often overlooked aspect of dog training, yet it is vital to your dog's development as a good, canine citizen. A well-socialized dog can interact with people and other pets without becoming afraid or aggressive. Socialization is teaching your Akita that others

FUN FACT
Popularity

Akitas are the 47th most popular breed in the United States according to the American Kennel Club.

will not hurt him, and that he can relax in the presence of strangers. This process can also teach an Akita how to play nicely with children and with other dogs.

Because Akitas tend to be wary of strangers and are not always friendly with other dogs, socialization is necessary at an early age. If you purchase a puppy, begin this process after your dog has had his vaccinations or around the four to eight-month mark. If you have adopted an older Akita, you should still work on your dog's social skills even though this process is most effective in puppies. You may feel overwhelmed by the thought of adding another type of training to your list of things to do while your dog is young, but do not put it off! Teaching socialization skills at an early age is one of the best things you can do to set your Akita up for a happy adulthood!

Greeting New Human Friends

Akitas tend to be protective of their owners, which can make it hard to take your dog in public or to have visitors in your home. This protective characteristic may be a prized trait for an owner that wants a reliable house alarm, but if the behavior turns into a serious fear or a distrust of strangers, it can be very upsetting. The ideal situation is for your Akita to be friendly and not aggressive toward others unless you instruct him to react otherwise. Socialization can train your dog that other people of all shapes and sizes are usually nothing to fear.

To begin this process, introduce your pup to trusted friends and family members by asking them to come to your house and to interact with your dog. Ask them to act calm around your dog and to allow your Akita to come to them, not the other way around. When your Akita is ready, he will sniff and approach your friends; when that happens, ask your visitors give your dog a treat. If he accepts the treat, have your visitor give your dog a pat on the head, too.

If your dog is nervous, do not force him to interact with these unfamiliar people. Let him watch the situation from a distance until he is ready to relate

Photo Courtesy
of Ben McBride

to these individuals and to accept treats from them. Always create positive interactions around your dog, so he knows that he has nothing to fear.

To take this training a step further, you may even ask strangers on the street to help you with your training. When you approach someone on a daily walk, ask if they would be willing to hand your puppy a treat. Give them one of your treats to use and keep an eye on your dog to make sure he is being nice in response. Try this approach with a variety of people, so when you socialize your dog with random people, he will be less likely to judge the individuals or to be afraid of an individual based solely on their appearance.

If you have kids in your household, this is also an appropriate time to teach them how to behave around a dog. Children are sometimes excitable in different situations, which can cause a nervous dog to become even more fearful. Instruct children to speak softly around your Akita and to not make too many sudden movements; explain why this is the best choice for everyone. Teach them how to gently pet a dog's back, and tell them to avoid the eyes, ears, mouth, and tail, which can be a sensitive area for the dog. Remind children to never poke or hit a dog because they might instinctively snap or growl to defend themselves. Also, show children how dogs greet people by using their nose and their sense of smell. Explain that once a dog has had the chance to sniff out the stranger, he may be receptive to gentle petting - away from the face.

Even after instructing a child, the most mild-mannered dogs should be supervised when there are young children present because both dogs and young children can be unpredictable. The last thing you want is for any member of your household to get hurt!

When it comes to socialization, start slowly and build your way up to more frequent interactions with people. If your dog is not immediately receptive to the idea, do not give up on him. Akitas are naturally more wary of strangers than other dogs so keep creating positive interactions to show your Akita there is nothing to worry about.

Socializing with Other Dogs

Akitas tend to be the happiest in homes where they are the only pet. However, this does not mean they cannot join a household with pets or they cannot play with other dogs. It will take a lot of work to get your Akita feeling comfortable around other pets, but it is possible.

As with human socialization, start slowly and increase the time you allow your dog to interact with other dogs. If you are working on socializing your new puppy, make sure you incorporate plenty of time apart from his canine siblings. When animals are forced to be together constantly (like brothers and sisters) and if they become stressed, they might feel trapped and might be more likely to lash out and snap at each other.

To prevent injury or added stress, make sure every dog has their own "quiet space" to go to when they feel overwhelmed. For example, you might use baby gates in several doorways of your home to give each dog a section of the house where they can go and relax.

*Photo Courtesy
of Chelsea Purdy*

Even if your Akita gets along with your other dogs, it is still a good idea to supervise all pets as much as possible when they are together. Animals give off vibes and messages that are virtually imperceptible to humans. Your pets can be happily playing one moment and fighting the next...and you might never feel the mood change! If you are supervising your pets, you will be quick to break up any fights or mitigate any tension between them before any pets get hurt.

If your Akita is your only pet, you will still want to work on his socialization skills. You can accomplish this by taking part in group training classes or by taking trips to the dog park, which can be fun for both of you if your dog is comfortable around other dogs.

Also, walks in popular dog-walking areas and trips to the vet will be much easier if your dog does not become alarmed at the sight of another dog. Start early in your dog's life with socialization but make sure your dog is current on his vaccinations before exposing him to other dogs.

To begin, take your dog to a dog park and keep him on a leash, close to your side. Many dog parks have a small dog section, so your puppy will not have to hold his own with the big dogs. Reinforce good behavior by giving him treats when he remains calm around the other dogs and dog owners. Let him sniff other dogs – that is how dogs introduce themselves. If your dog seems interested in playing and does not appear to be overly fearful or aggressive, you can take him off the leash and see how he plays with other dogs.

It is sometimes difficult to distinguish between rough-dog play and fighting between two or more canines. Play can be rough without causing injury; however, it is important to know the signs of aggression in dogs when you see it. Growling, baring of the teeth, hair standing up between the dog's shoulders, and a stiff tail are all signs that aggression will soon follow. If a fight does break out, it can be extremely dangerous for you to break things up by putting your body between the two fighting dogs.

Instead, try to move your Akita away from the other dog(s) by pulling him backward by his legs until you can safely reach for the collar. If you stick your hand into the middle of a fight to grab the collar, you risk a situation where your dog might think you are another attacking dog, which can lead to unintended injuries.

If you are breaking up a fight between your dogs at home, some trainers suggest holding a large object between the dogs, such as a baking sheet, which will keep the dogs from fighting. An object of this size is large enough to keep you out of reach of a snarling dog. Once your dogs are safely separated, move one dog away from the other dog and give both plenty of time to cool off.

Socializing with Other Animals

Teaching your Akita to get along with other types of pets can present additional challenges. Akitas have a moderate prey drive, so they may see a small critter and instinctively want to chase it. For the safety of small, pocket-pet-type animals, keep all pet cages secure and out of reach of your dog. An

Photo Courtesy of Natasha Grant

Akita will likely not understand the difference between a pet hamster and a wild squirrel; they might want to catch any small animal running loose! If you usually allow your pet rodent, lizard, or bird to roam the house, strongly consider placing your pet in a cage or tank where it cannot be bothered by your Akita.

Cats and dogs can be friends, but cats may also look like prey to an Akita. When socializing, never force your cat and dog to interact; instead, let them sniff each other on their own time but in your presence. Give your Akita treats when he is kind to your cat and always correct rough behavior between the two animals with a loud noise – then, redirect their actions.

Avoid letting your Akita feel rewarded by the fun of chasing another pet. If your dog seems overly excited, put the other pet in a safe place and redirect your dog's attention; always make sure each pet has a safe place to go. A tall cat tree works well to keep your kitten out of reach, or a room with a baby gate in the doorway may allow your cat to hop to safety to avoid your dog. Dogs need safe spaces, too, so crate your Akita if you are unable to supervise your pets so he does not get scratched by an annoyed cat!

Supervision of our dog is absolutely necessary, especially in the early days of training. The last thing you want is for your dog to give into their canine instincts and to hurt one of your pets because he instinctively thought it was prey. Over time, your pets may learn to get along through gentle introduction and positive reinforcement. However, if your pets do not get along, you may want to consider rehoming a pet or returning your Akita to the breeder or shelter. It can be hard to make that decision, but it is in everyone's best interest in order to have a peaceful household.

Pack Mentality

Some dog trainers believe domesticated dogs still ascribe to the rules of their ancestor's hierarchy while other trainers believe modern dogs are so far removed from their past they abide by other rules. If you have multiple dogs, you may find one takes on the role of the leader while others are more submissive. This does not necessarily mean one dog is aggressive and the other is frightened; it may just mean they take on separate roles in their "pack." Regardless of their social order, you will want to be seen as the leader of the pack.

While your dogs may police each other's actions, you want to have the final word when it comes to correcting bad behaviors. To enforce your role as the pack leader, some trainers recommend walking through a doorway before your dog and eating supper before giving your dog his food. These can be small gestures, but they may help your dog earn your respect.

Photo Courtesy of Gustavo Lomeli

Raising Multiple Akitas

When you purchase your Akita puppy, you may be tempted to buy another pup. While it can be fun to have multiple dogs in the house, consider first why you want to buy two dogs. Some people assume having a second dog will entertain the first, but it does not always work out that way. With two puppies, you will have twice the expenses, twice the messes to clean, and twice the bathroom trips outside. Raising one puppy can be a challenge - imagine raising two at the same time! If you are an experienced dog owner and you spend a lot of time at home, you may be up for the challenge. Otherwise, you might risk finding yourself financially, physically, and mentally overwhelmed by dog care!

One alternative is to raise one Akita puppy; then, buy a second Akita puppy when the first one reaches adulthood. This will give you some experience before you raise the second pup. Also, you will make good use of all of your puppy's hand-me-down supplies.

Another option is to find an Akita rescue that will allow you to foster dogs. This allows you to care for multiple dogs without the long-term commitment of ownership plus you might save a dog's life and prepare him for his future home by fostering him...always a rewarding feeling!

If you give in and choose to buy two pups from the same litter, beware of littermate syndrome. This is a behavioral trait some trainers and owners see when two dogs from the same litter go to the same home.

The siblings can be more difficult to raise than puppies from different litters because they become codependent and display unwanted behaviors, such as severe separation anxiety or an inability to behave during training. If your two puppies show this syndrome, they might distract each other during training to the point where neither dog learns anything; this results in you becoming frustrated with both dogs that cannot be apart but that cannot behave when they are together either. For this reason, some dog experts suggest buying puppies from two different litters if you decide to raise two puppies at the same time.

Socializing your dog to be comfortable around people and other animals is an easy way to ensure your dog feels safe around others, which translates into others feeling safe around your dog. By slowly introducing your Akita to trusted friends, other dogs and pets, and by reinforcing good behavior with treats, praise, and petting, you will see an enormous difference in your dog's and in your life. Starting socialization at an early age (before your Akita becomes an adult dog who may not trust others), is also ideal. Working on social skills throughout your dog's life will develop a calm, obedient, and all-around good doggy-citizen!

CHAPTER 8
Physical and Mental Exercise

"Akitas love to walk and hike with their family. I also like to train my dogs in Nose work and Scent work, as it is great mental stimulation. Really any dog sport helps to exercise their mind as well as body."

LINDA BACCO
Shogitai Akitas

Not only is exercise important for your dog's physical health, but it will also improve his mental health and his overall behavior. Without sufficient exercise, Akitas can gain excess weight, especially if they are eating more calories than they burn, which can put a huge strain on his body. Exercise can alleviate an overweight problem, and it can also be mentally stimulating for your dog, which helps his mind stay sharp and keeps him in a better mood. Another added benefit of exercise is your dog will behave better if he is too tired to be naughty or to be anxious. A tired dog is usually a good dog because exercise with fun activities burns energy and discourages destructive, doggy games. Akitas possess loads of playful energy so be creative with lively and spirited activities you can do together!

Exercise Requirements

Exercise requirements vary from dog to dog depending on age and temperament so adjust the activity level to suit your dog's specific needs. The average adult Akita will need about an hour of exercise per day, which can be split into several different activities. For instance, you can take your Akita on a short walk in the morning and another walk in the evening. Or you might split your exercise into short bouts of playtime in the backyard throughout the day. Your Akita does not care whether their daily exercise is spread throughout the day or is in one complete period of time...they will simply be happy exercising with you!

Keep in mind Akitas prefer certain types of weather more than others; they LOVE cold weather, so thirty minutes of play in your backyard after a snowstorm would be tons of fun for an Akita. Walks in freezing temperatures are no problem for this breed, either!

On the other hand, this breed can be sensitive to the heat. Spending too much time in the heat and the sun can result in heat illness. If you find yourself in the middle of a heatwave, try walking your Akita early in the morning before the temperatures rise or stay indoors and conduct playtime in the air conditioning. Remember to keep your outdoor exercise brief and take breaks for cold water along the way. If your Akita appears slow or sluggish during a walk, take a break in the shade before turning around to go home. You do not want to push your dog to walk too far when it is hot outside.

Activities to Do with Your Akita

Taking walks with your Akita is a great form of exercise, but there are lots of other things that you can do with your dog as well.

If you have a fenced backyard, there are tons of games you can play. For example, playing catch is a fun, easy game that requires nothing more than a ball. Tennis balls are a favorite for this game because they are soft but have enough weight to be thrown a long distance. Some dogs are naturals at catching a tennis ball while others are not, which means this can be a training session on how to catch a ball as well as being his daily exercise.

Once your dog has mastered that skill, try throwing a Frisbee to him to catch. Pet stores sell Frisbees that are made from soft materials, so your dog can easily catch them without getting hurt by an errant throw. In the winter, replace the tennis ball or Frisbee with snowballs and watch your Akita go crazy!

Fetch is another fun game that practices useful commands. Often times, dogs are able to chase after the ball, but do not want to give it back. Fetch requires your Akita to take an object, bring it to you, and to drop it. (These commands will be covered in a later chapter and can be particularly useful.) Once your dog has mastered the game of fetch, you will be able to wear him out with little effort on your part!

If you live near a body of water, you might try swimming with your Akita when it is too hot to go for a walk. Akitas are not necessarily known for their love of water, but if your dog does seem to enjoy being in the water, it might be an enjoyable way to beat the heat. Swimming is a low-impact form of exercise that burns a lot of energy. You can even incorporate a game of fetch into the swim.

When taking your dog to swim, slowly introduce him to water. Let him explore the water on his own terms, so he does not develop an aversion after being dunked. Always keep a close eye on your dog while he swims and consider fitting your swimmer with a doggy life jacket.

Knowing that Akitas love the snow, you might have success with different snow sports; have you ever heard of skijoring? Skijoring is a sport that is similar to a dog sled, but it is just one dog pulling one person on skis. If your sidewalks are too snowy for walks, you might try cross-country skiing or snowshoeing with your Akita. By adding sporting equipment to your playtime, and trying a sport such as skijoring, you will be creating added fun for you while your dog will be spending more time in the snow...something an Akita loves!

Finally, consider entering your dog in an Akita dog-club activity. After you register your pup in the American Kennel Club, you can begin competing in different events against other dogs. For example, if your dog loves obedience class, conformation and obedience in the ring can be a fun way to show off your pet's abilities.

If your Akita is energetic and athletic, two competitions, rally and agility, require dogs to go through a series of obstacles on a specific course in the ring. The American Akita Club even has a sport called "Barn Hunt" where dogs search through a barn, with bales of hay as obstacles, in order to find a rat, which is enclosed in a cage. This event highlights each dogs' tracking skills and is fun for dogs and owners alike. Even if you never enter any competition, you will still have fun if you incorporate these skills into your dog's daily exercise routine

To keep your dog entertained and always on his toes, you might switch up the activities you do with him. Even changing your walking route can keep things exciting for your Akita because there will be new sights, sounds, and smells to discover along the way. Or you can make the game of fetch even more challenging by going to a dog park and using a ball launcher for even more distance, or you could add a new ball or toy to the game instead of the usual tennis ball. Whatever daily exercise you introduce to your Akita, always remember to monitor your dog during each activity to make sure he is feeling well and having fun.

Photo Courtesy
of Charlie Pound

Photo Courtesy of Katie Russell

Mental Exercise

Mental exercise is an underrated part of your dog's overall wellbeing and is sometimes overlooked by dog owners. If not mentally stimulated, dogs can get bored and show unwanted behavioral issues. If senior dogs do not receive ample mental exercise, they may also suffer from cognitive issues. Luckily, there are a lot of things you can do with your dog to keep his mind sharp and to keep him entertained.

FUN FACT
A Gift for the Baby

In Japan, the first gift that a baby will receive is often a small statue of an Akita dog. This statue is meant to represent health, longevity, and happiness.

A lot of the physical exercise and training you do with your Akita can also be considered mental exercise. Even a walk around the block works your dog's mind because he is gathering so much information by using his senses. For example, a game of fetch requires your dog to read your physical cues and utilize your commands. Obedience training requires your Akita to use his brain to figure out what you want him to do in order to receive a reward. Simply fulfilling every-day requirements of dog ownership will help your dog stay entertained and sharp.

However, there is more you can do to keep your dog's brain active even when you are away from home. When you leave your Akita home alone, try leaving fun toys for him to explore! Puzzle toys are especially enticing for dogs because they deliver a reward when your dog completes the puzzle. Some toys require your dog to bounce a ball exactly right in order to receive a treat while others contain sliding doors and levers that your dog must move with his snout in order to win the prize. Even leaving out sturdy bones with tasty fillings while you are away will give your dog something to do until you get home.

You can also work your dog's mind during playtime together. Some dogs love to play hide and seek, which can also be a fun game for your whole family. To play, have your dog sit and stay in one part of the house while you hide in another room and call your dog. Your Akita should run toward the direction of your voice and sniff around until they find you. One variation on this game is to hide your dog's favorite toy and teach him to find it. Of course, a loving hug and verbal praise when found is a must!

Since this breed loves the snow, you can incorporate mental exercise when playing outdoors in wintery weather, too. With fresh snow on the

Photo Courtesy
of Chelsea Purdy

ground, hide your dog's favorite treats or one of his toys in a snowbank and watch as he explores your yard to uncover them. Or try hiding yourself behind a snowdrift and see if your Akita can sniff you out. He will find this type of play both fun and rewarding, and it might keep him occupied for quite some time, which will ultimately prevent annoying or destructive behaviors, too!

Exercise is important for both your dog's overall health and for your sanity as a pet owner! Akitas are energetic and playful dogs, so sitting around the house with no physical or mental exercise is hard on this type of dog. You should aim for at least one hour of exercise a day mixed with plenty of play and mental stimulation. Remember when exercising, be sure your Akita has access to cool water and to shade when needed. Keep your activities fun and fresh, and you will both look forward to the time you are active together!

CHAPTER 9
Training Your Akita

"My biggest tip on training your Akita can be done inside your own home. This easy tip will help establish a pecking order in your pack. Never let them go through a door in front of you. Have the dog stop and allow you to go first. When you go on a walk, have him stop in let you go through the door first. This simple task will teach him respect and he will see you as the master of the house."

CAROL FRIEDMAN
Sovereign Akitas

Obedience training is a necessary part of being an owner of an Akita. Without this type of training, you will find your dog difficult to manage, which will lead to frustration for both of you! Akitas are easily trained dogs as long as they practice on a regular basis and receive lots of positive reinforcement. A well-trained Akita is a pleasure to own; however, training requires a lot of work and knowledge about how dogs learn. This chapter will explain how dogs can be trained to perform certain tasks, so you can use this knowledge to teach your Akita whatever you please!

Setting Clear Expectations

Consistency and clear expectations are key when it comes to training your dog, especially when you are training your Akita to work with other members of the family. Dogs learn through repetition and reward, not through reasoning; therefore, consistency in commands and in response or praise need to be the same no matter who is giving the instruction. For instance, you might not mind when your

CELEBRITY DOGS

Tyson

Sarah Michelle Gellar, of *Buffy the Vampire Slayer* fame, owned an Akita named Tyson. Gellar described Tyson as "the most beautiful, the most tender, the most gentle." Tyson was exceedingly gentle with children and unfazed by the antics of Gellar's other dogs, particularly her Maltese named Thor.

Akita jumps on you, but you do not want him to jump on other people who come into your home. Since dogs are not able to distinguish differences between what is and what is not appropriate behavior, they must be conditioned to behave the same in similar situations.

If you train your dog to not jump on people, they will avoid jumping on anyone they encounter. If you allow them to jump up in some situations but not others, your dog will struggle to make the distinction between acceptable and unacceptable reactions for jumping up. When you make rules for your Akita's behavior, try to make your instructions simple and clear so your dog behaves appropriately every time.

If you are training your Akita with a family member, the two of you will need to work together to keep the training consistent. For example, if you use the word "Yes" for your positive verbal cue and your partner uses "Good", then your dog will be receiving two different cues. Dogs do not know that "Yes" and "Good" mean the same thing, and they might become confused by these different commands. Or, if you use the word "Off" when you want your dog to jump down from furniture but a family member uses the word "Down" for the same command, you will be giving your dog two different commands for the same action.

You may even find your training partner and you have conflicting philosophies when it comes to training dogs. You may want to use a no-pull harness when walking your dog, and your partner might want to train your Akita with a regular collar. The best way to remain on the same page with other family members is to attend training classes together. Many classes give more instruction to dog owners on the correct way to train their dog than they do on instructing the dog itself.

Using Operant Conditioning

A psychological concept, called operant conditioning, is the theory that your dog will associate behaviors with positive or negative consequences; this is the way most dogs learn. When you train a dog using operant conditioning, you teach him to act immediately when he hears a command. If he successfully matches an action to your command, he is rewarded; the rewards provide incentive to repeat that action. With enough repetition and reward, your dog will automatically follow your command when he hears the appropriate word. Dogs do not necessarily understand the meaning of command words, but they can recognize certain sounds and connect them to a behavior.

A dog's behavior can either receive a reward or a punishment. A good behavior is strengthened through a positive reward while some theories

Photo Courtesy
of Petre Trandafirescu

73

state bad behaviors can be eliminated through punishment. However, it has been proven dogs learn best through positive reinforcement – not negative.

While a child may learn from receiving a punishment for an action, dogs' brains are not complex enough to learn from their mistakes in the same way humans do. Granted, a punishment can deter certain behaviors, but it can also cause even worse behavior. For example, yelling at an Akita for having an accident on the carpet is an unpleasant punishment for a dog. Instead of learning from that punishment and only going to the bathroom outside, your dog may completely avoid going to the bathroom around you in general, leading him to hide his accidents around your house.

Rewarding all positive behaviors is much more effective when it comes to conditioning your dog. It is amazing what you can train your dog to do when you understand the basics of operant conditioning.

The Best Reinforcements for Your Akita

"You can't drill them. You need to be clear when training them, practice a few times but don't continue to drill exercises. Many Akitas will start to improvise and put their own spin on what is being taught."

LINDA BACCO
Shogitai Akitas

While there are several different methods of positive reinforcements, praising a dog with a treat tends to be the go-to for most dog owners because they are easy to give out, and dogs go crazy for them! In fact, many food-driven dogs will do anything to get a tasty treat.

Small training treats come in assorted flavors and are all very enticing to a dog. Moist treats are especially effective because the moisture in the treat gives off a stronger scent than a dry biscuit. If your dog is particularly stubborn, a high-value treat can make training easier. Perhaps something special like a small piece of hot dog or tuna will get your dog to pay attention to you! Whatever you use when your dog successfully completes a command, give a verbal cue, such as "Yes" and give him the treat.

When starting to teach your dog a new command, give him a treat every time he completes the command. Eventually, you should switch to an interval or random reward schedule. For instance, instead of every time he follows your command, give him a treat every third time so he is weaned off a treat system to one of verbal praise. Your dog will start to follow your command without treats, which shows a maturity and responsibility for simply wanting to please his owner.

Unfortunately, not all dogs respond to treats; some prefer play as their choice of reward. Recognizing good behavior by initiating playtime with your pup is an appropriate alternative to handing out treats though it is not as easy or precise. Still, if your dog is especially toy-driven and is not interested in food, this can be a valuable tool for your training toolbox. If your Akita successfully completes a command, reward him with some sort of play. For example, if your dog comes to you on command, give him his favorite squeaky toy or play a quick game of tug. It takes some creativity to find ways to reward your dog with toys, but it can be an effective way to keep your Akita motivated and having fun at the same time.

Some owners and trainers swear by clicker training because this method is easy and exact. A clicker is a small, handheld tool that clicks when the trainer pushes the button. The "click" becomes the reward after you condition your dog to associate the sound with a small treat. To begin, click the clicker and give your dog a treat. After enough time, your dog will relate the sound to the treats. When training, click the clicker when your dog does something good. This is a useful tool because it can reward your dog the instant he does what you ask him to do. It is also easier than carrying around a bag of treats, and your dog will not gain weight by responding to a clicker!

Training with Positivity

The importance of positivity during dog training cannot be overstated. Not only will your dog be happier with positive reinforcement, but dogs learn commands best when they are rewarded for good behavior. Whenever your dog does something good, give him some sort of reward, whether it is a treat, a toy, or praise and petting. Your dog needs to make positive connections with behaviors in order to repeat them. If your dog thinks training is a fun and challenging time that yields lots of tasty treats, he will definitely be eager to learn!

However, if he is constantly receiving punishments for making the wrong choices during training time, he may learn to hate training and will not be interested in learning new commands at all.

Akitas are intelligent creatures, and they love to be involved in challenging activities; however, if they are not motivated or engaged in an activity, they will likely make their own rules! To keep your Akita involved, try training for short periods of time, around twenty minutes, and end each session with something your dog loves, such as a game of catch or a special treat. If you train for too long, your pup will lose interest and his mind (and body) will start to wander. Or practice commands in different settings, which should keep your dog's training new and fresh.

Dog training can be frustrating, especially if your Akita is acting stubbornly or is not picking up commands as quickly as you would like. Your dog can sense negative emotions, and he will not be successful if he feels your annoyance. Showing frustration can also be seen as negative reinforcement by your dog and will impair your dog's ability to learn commands. If you feel you are starting to become aggravated with the training, take a step back and end the session for the day. Return to training when both you and your dog are ready to have a positive experience – one which will lead to new experiences while having fun with one another.

Hiring a Trainer

Every dog owner and their dog should take a training course at least once in their life. Classes are just as educational for the owner as they are for the dog – maybe even more so! You will learn about a variety of breeds of dog (and about your Akita) from someone with a lot of experience with the topic. Classes give you the opportunity to work with your dog while a knowledgeable trainer is right there to give you help and advice. You will also gain a valuable resource with whom you can talk whenever you are having issues with your Akita.

Photo Courtesy
of Stephane Michaud

When deciding what type of training class in which to enroll, you will find there are many different types of classes being offered. One example is you might choose between group classes and private classes. Group classes are less expensive than private classes, and the group setting allows your dog to socialize and to become comfortable around unfamiliar people and dogs.

Private classes are great if you want specialized help or if your schedule makes going to group classes difficult. Private classes will be more expensive, but you will be able to work on your Akita's behavioral issues and training goals without having to follow a group lesson plan.

The skills learned in dog training classes also vary. Many owners enroll their puppy in a puppy class around the six-month mark. From there, obedience classes range in difficulty, progressing from basic to advanced. Then, there are specific training classes that teach your dog new skills. Some of these specific classes focus on agility, while others can help your dog become licensed as a therapy dog. After obedience classes, you can enroll your Akita in classes that best suit his personality and skills.

If you are looking for a group class, oftentimes pet stores have trainers that work out of their store to present classes, or your city might have a dog club where different trainers give classes directly in the organization's building. You might also search for independent dog trainers, or you can ask other dog owners for a recommendation for either type of instruction. Finally, when checking out a trainer's website, look for a trainer that mentions positivity in their training practice.

Appropriate and early training is an important part of raising an Akita. Not only does training teach your Akita how to live in your home, but it keeps your dog's mind sharp and active at the same time. An untrained dog can cause a lot of tension in your household, whereas a trained dog is a pleasure to live with! Once you understand the basics behind dog training, you can apply that knowledge so your dog learns to follow a multitude of commands.

Remember, training should be positive. If you find yourself getting frustrated, take a break or work with a professional dog trainer to help you unlock your Akita's full potential!

CHAPTER 10
Commands

O nce you understand operant conditioning, you can apply that theory to any command you choose. When you train a dog, you are rewarding good behavior and pairing that good behavior with a verbal cue. With repetition, your dog becomes conditioned to automatically perform the desired action when you give the cue. This chapter will give you step-by-step instructions for some common dog commands. This chapter is split into two sections - basic commands and advanced commands.

There are several basic commands all dogs should learn – commands that can save your dog's life. For instance, if your Akita escapes your yard and runs towards the road, being able to call your dog to come back is an invaluable skill. Or if your dog picks up a dangerous object, the ability to drop it on cue can prevent illness or injury. Even training your dog to walk properly beside you can improve the lives of both you and your dog because you

Photo Courtesy
of Debhorah Di Rosa

will be able to exercise without constantly fighting your Akita. Once you have mastered these important basic commands, you can move on to more advanced commands, such as shake or spin. These extra commands have little practical use, but they can keep your dog occupied and are a lot of fun to show off!

Basic Commands

Sit

This is typically the first command every dog learns. "Sit" is useful for controlling your Akita and for keeping him still. You can practice this command while waiting to cross the street, when someone comes to the door, or while talking to people at the park.

To teach this command, start with your dog facing you. Hold a treat in front of his nose, then slowly move it up and back. He will naturally sit in order to reach the treat. The second his bottom touches the floor say, "Yes! Good sit!" and give him the treat. Eventually, your dog will understand the "Sit" command means he is supposed to sit until given further instruction.

When you are ready for your dog to stand up say, "Okay," and have him stand and come toward you and then give him another treat. Repeat these steps until he connects your verbal command to the action. Always give your dog a treat if he correctly follows your command.

If you are having difficulty getting your dog into the Sit position, you might apply light pressure above the base of his tail to gently move him into a sitting position. You are not forcing your Akita to sit down, but you are gently reminding him what you mean by "Sit."

FUN FACT
Instagram Famous

Possibly Instagram's most famous Akita is Malcolm the Akita from Bordeaux, France. Malcolm can be found on Instagram with the username @malcolm_the_akita and has amassed over 83,000 followers on the social media platform. Malcolm's owner, May, maintains a blog to chronicle Malcolm's modeling career and picturesque adventures.

Also, if your dog is not responding to your command, do not repeat your words until he appears ready to listen. Say, "Sit," once, then if he does not respond, either move the treat in front of his face, or apply light pressure on his bottom until he catches on.

Down

This command puts your dog in a prone position and is the next step after teaching the Sit command. The word "Down" will keep your dog under your control longer than "Sit." For instance, you might have your dog sit when you need him to be still for just a moment - if you need to clip a leash on him. In contrast, you might put your dog in a down position when you need him to relax while you answer the door.

To teach this command, start with your dog in the Sit position. Then, hold a treat in front of the dog's nose, lower the treat to the ground, and your dog's

Photo Courtesy
of Chelsea Roth

head should follow it until his chin is near the ground. You can also tuck your fingers into your dog's collar or gently apply tension to his leash, so his head lowers to the floor. When his elbows touch the ground say, "Yes! Good down!" and give him the treat. Never use excessive force to move your dog to the ground. Instead, any pressure should merely guide him into the desired position.

Stay

This command is necessary if you have an Akita that gets easily distracted. If your dog can sit and stay, you will not have to worry about him running off if you have to drop the leash for a moment. This command is also useful if you want to play hide and seek with your dog. Begin by teaching this command in the Sit position, then move to the Down position.

To teach this command, start with your dog sitting beside you, facing the same direction. Say, "Stay," and hold your hand in front of his face. If he does not move after a brief moment, reward him. Once he has mastered that, try walking in a circle around your dog. The second he moves, put him back into the Sit position and try again. Do not reward your dog if he moves; instead, give lots of praise and rewards if he stays still.

Once your dog has the basic idea, create more distance between him and you. Have him stay while you back away and then return to his side. Or you can have him stay and then call him to you. Each time add more distance and distractions to test your dog's ability to listen and to trust you. In the beginning, set your dog up for success by keeping the wait time and the distance between you short. As your dog's skills develop, add more space, time, and distractions.

Come

This recall command can be extremely useful when a sudden danger appears or when you just want your dog to come inside at the end of the day. Akitas may try to chase other animals, so you will want a strong recall if your dog cannot suppress the instinct to run. If you catch your dog in the process of running off, a strong recall can keep him from straying too far, which could potentially save his life. The end goal is to have your dog stop immediately and to return to you no matter how focused he is on his adventure.

To teach this command, with a treat, excitedly say your dog's name. When he comes running to you to investigate say, "Yes! Good come!" and reward him. If your dog naturally comes to you, reward him in the same way as if you purposefully called him. Increase the distance and continue calling your dog to you and rewarding with his favorite treats.

Over time, you want to be able to touch your dog's collar without him jumping back and running away. Some dogs love to be chased, so you will want to make sure your dog will come to you without trying to get you to give chase. Adding the sit command will help you hold onto him in case of emergency. Once your dog begins to understand "Come," try adding a "Sit" and "Stay" command to keep him from dashing off again to play.

Sometimes, owners call their dog because they have done something naughty. When this happens, the owner's voice is usually harsh and angry. This teaches the dog if he responds to "Come," he will be punished. Only use the Come command in positive situations, or your dog may not obey your wishes when it really counts. You want your dog to think coming to you is the best thing in the world and that he will be met with lots of love and affection!

Photo Courtesy
of Charlotte Arcand

Off

It may be cute when your Akita puppy jumps up to greet you when you walk into the door, but it can be annoying or frightening if your full-grown Akita does the same thing to a visitor! To discourage this bad habit, train your Akita to understand the "Off" command. Remember, there is a difference between the "Down" and the "Off" command so make sure you use the right cue word for the right command.

One way you can teach this command is to say, "Off," and to turn your back to your dog as he is jumping up on you. By ignoring his actions, he will not get the reward of attention - which he is hoping for – and will only receive his treat after all four paws return to the floor.

If turning your back on your dog and ignoring his actions when he jumps does not change his behavior, you can try to teach this command with your Akita on his leash. Step on the leash so there is not enough slack so your dog CANNOT jump up. When he tries to jump, he will get pulled back down to the ground by his leash. Not only will this discourage the jumping, but it will allow you to reward your dog when his feet are back on the ground.

Drop It

This skill may not be on the top of the list of basic skills owners teach their new dogs, but it can save a dog's life in an emergency. Dogs are naturally curious, so they are inclined to put their mouths on things they find enticing or interesting. Many times, the things they find can make them sick, such as a rotting animal or a forbidden food. Sometimes it is also worth it to teach this command just so you can successfully play fetch and know your dog will Drop It when you want to retrieve the ball from his mouth for another round.

If you play catch or fetch with your Akita, this is a perfect way to teach this command. Toss a ball and let him catch it in his mouth. If he drops the ball on his own, praise this behavior and say, "Good drop!" If your dog is not so willing to relinquish his toy, hold a treat in front of his face. He will likely drop the ball so there is room for a treat in his mouth. Praise this behavior in the same way you would if he dropped the ball without prompting.

For play-driven dogs, your pup may just want an opportunity to tug at the toy before dropping it. As long as your dog eventually drops it, a quick tug can be a good reward for bringing an object to you. Eventually, you will be able to tell your dog to pick up an object and to put it back down without any rewards. Trust me...if you ever catch your dog with something gross in his mouth, you will be glad he learned this command!

Walk

Since Akitas require a large amount of exercise, taking daily walks is a necessary part of life. An Akita is a strong dog that can pull you around by his leash and can make walks very unpleasant if he does not willingly walk by your side. Walking calmly on a leash is not intuitive to most dogs; they would much rather run ahead or lag behind as they sniff and explore every new scent. The object here is to train your dog how to "Heel." This means your dog walks close to your heel while on a loose leash.

When going for a walk, always walk with your dog on your left side. This routine teaches your dog he belongs in a specific place and should not be wandering anywhere. Hold the end of the leash in your right hand and slide your left hand halfway down the leash to keep your dog close. That way, if your dog gets out of position, the tension on the leash will correct him.

To train your dog to stay close to your left hip, hold a treat in your right hand, guiding him forward with the treat. If he walks with you, give him tons of praise and treats. If your dog looks at you for direction at any point, make a big deal about what a wonderful job he is doing. You want your dog to walk with you, rather than attempt to lead you. This is especially important so your dog cannot easily pull you around. If your full-sized dog pulls hard enough and he will not walk calmly at your side, you might very easily become injured.

Akitas are strong dogs and may not care if there is tension on the leash. Instead, they might surge ahead anyway, even to the point where the collar and short leash hurts their throat. One way to alert your dog that this behavior is not acceptable is to stop in your tracks the moment he starts to pull. Over time, he will figure out he can only receive his reward if he walks with a loose leash. If that is not enough, do an abrupt about-turn every time he pulls. It may be a while before you actually go anywhere, but it will teach your Akita that you are in charge of the walk.

Some owners will switch to a harness, instead of a buckle collar, for fear the dog might hurt himself if he keeps straining on the leash. However, this will sometimes simply allow a dog to pull even harder because a harness does not apply pressure to his throat. Instead of changing collars, you should eventually be able to walk your Akita with a buckle collar.

If walking on a leash is a problem for your dog, talk to a trainer about how you can rectify the situation. Since Akitas are so big and strong, you might want someone with experience to help you remedy the problem.

It is easy for bad walking habits to be accidently reinforced, so it is important to be strict when it comes to leash training. Do not allow your dog to pull you with the leach, simply to get in his exercise. You may find yourself

Photo Courtesy
of Nathanael Wilson

spinning in circles for a few walks, but it is better than allowing your dog to drag you wherever he wants to go on every walk in the future.

Never go on a walk without plenty of treats because every walk is full of training opportunities. Do not give up on walking outdoors simply because your Akita has a mind of his own and is resistant to training. Keep working at it until your dog walks calmly by your side with a loose leash and allows you to lead him - not the other way around!

Advanced Commands

Take it/Leave it

These are two commands that can be useful when you want your dog to pick something up or to ignore something enticing. They can also be paired with the "Drop It" command.

To train your dog to pick something up, place a treat in front of him and say, "Take It." Naturally, he will want to take the treat. Give him praise and affection when he takes the treat once the command had been given. After he successfully picks up a treat on cue several times, replace the treat with a toy and continue giving your dog the "Take It" command. When he picks up the toy, give it a tug or give him a treat and praise him for following your directions.

To train your dog to "Leave It," put a treat on the floor in front of him, and tell him to "Leave It." He will naturally try to pick up the treat; when he does, cover the treat with your hand. Repeat this process until he no longer automatically reaches for the treat. When this occurs say, "Good Leave It," and give him the treat. Continue this practice until your dog will wait for you to release him from "Leave It" before taking the treat. Once he has mastered both commands, you can practice by placing treats nearby (or even on his paws) and tell him to "Leave It." See how long your dog can stay still before you allow him to take the treats.

The command "Leave It" can also be useful in scenarios when your dog is interested in something you want him to ignore. For instance, he may find a dead animal during a walk that he wants to roll in. By telling him to "Leave It," he should turn his attention back to you. When he does, you should reinforce the good behavior with a treat.

You can also use this command when you want your dog to leave other animals alone. If you have other pets in the house and your Akita is pestering them, tell your dog to "Leave It," and reward him when he stops the behavior.

Shake/High Five

This is a simple dog trick that is easy to teach and is lots of fun to show off! Begin by having your dog sit facing you; hold a treat in your hand near the paw you want him to lift. He will likely sniff and push your hand with his nose out of curiosity but do not give him the treat just yet. When he cannot force the treat out of your hand, he will use his paw to try and open your hand. If he tries to use his paw in any way say, "Shake," and give him the treat.

Continue this until your dog responds to the command by lifting his paw for you to grab. If he does not respond to the treat in your hand, you may try poking at his foot or leg until he lifts his paw. Always praise and reward this behavior when it happens.

To teach the "High Five" variation, simply hold the treat up higher. For "Shake," hold your hand around his elbow height. For "High Five," hold the treat at his shoulder height. This will cause the dog to raise his paw a little higher. As soon as his paw makes contact with the palm of your hand, give him the treat. Once you have taught your dog both tricks, practice switching between "Shake" and "High Five" for an added challenge.

Crawl

This trick is cute and may be incorporated into a homemade obstacle course or agility run.

To teach this command, start your dog in a "Down" position and hold a treat on the ground, just

Photo Courtesy of Pete Bissinger

out of his reach. Your dog will start to move forward to get the treat. If he stands up, do not give him the reward. Try again until your dog crawls forward a few steps...then, reward him. Once he gets the hang of it, increase the distance you expect him to crawl. For added difficulty, have your dog crawl under an object or between your legs.

Spin

Getting your Akita to twirl around for a treat makes him look like he is dancing but if the trick is done correctly, he will "Spin" without jumping up or putting his paws on you.

To teach this command, begin with your dog facing you, a few feet away, in a standing position. Holding a treat in your hand, call your dog to you. When your dog is about to take the treat from you, bring the treat in toward your body and then out and around in a circle. Your dog will follow your hand and spin as you make a circle with your arm.

It is best for your dog to get a little momentum when going into the spin, so be sure he stands several feet away from you before you call him to you. Keeping a good distance will help him build up enough speed to complete the turn. When he has mastered right turns, try left turns. You can also alternate directions or add other movements into your dance.

CHAPTER 11
Traveling with Your Akita

Your Akita is part of your family, so it is only natural that you will want to take him everywhere you go! However, traveling with a dog can become a stressful situation, for both you and for your dog. To keep traveling as easy as possible for everyone, plan ahead, stay organized, and keep your dog's safety in mind. This chapter will outline how to take your dog on trips with you, and how to leave your dog at home if he cannot come along.

Photo Courtesy of Suzye Landry

Photo Courtesy of Elsy Mattar

Dog Crates and Car Restraints

Proper car restraints are necessary whenever you take your Akita on a drive in order to keep your dog safe. First, an unrestrained dog, while riding in a car, can be a huge distraction for the driver. You do not want a dog wandering around the car and demanding your attention when you are driving.

In the event of an accident, your dog can also become seriously injured if he is wandering freely in the back seat. Even braking too suddenly can cause an unrestrained dog to fly forward, which could cause him injury. Just as with humans, you should always be sure your dog is safely restrained while riding in the car – for all the same reasons.

Fortunately, there are several options when restraining a dog in your car. Since Akitas are larger dogs, you need a crate or restraint system that is meant for a dog his size. If your Akita is crate trained, a crate can be secured in your car to provide protection for your dog. Not only will a crate keep your dog from flying around, but the rigid walls will protect him from flying debris or from blunt force injuries if they should occur.

If you do not use a crate or if your car is too small to hold a crate, seatbelts paired with harnesses work well to keep your dog in his seat. Dog seatbelts can be purchased at pet stores, and they simply clip into your car's seatbelts before attaching to the dog's harness. When choosing a car restraint system, make sure that it will protect your dog during a crash. Any restraint that could allow your dog to move from seat to seat or to fly into the windshield should not be used.

Preparing Your Dog for Car Rides

While some dogs love car rides, others become fearful at the mere thought of riding in a car...to the point of carsickness. To ensure your car rides go smoothly, there are a few ways you can make your dog feel more at home while in your vehicle.

First, consider your dog's basic needs before going on a trip. Has your dog eaten and had enough water before your drive? Has he used the bathroom before getting in the car? Take your dog on a long walk before you start your drive, so he does not have any excess nervous energy.

Before taking a long trip, practice riding in the car with him. Dogs learn through their experiences, so if your dog has had good experiences in a car, your trip will be a breeze. When beginning this training, take your dog on short drives while speaking to him in a calm, reassuring voice; give him lots of treats when the ride is over. You might also consider playing with your dog and his special toy upon returning home as a reward for good behavior.

Gradually, increase the length of your car rides and continue to give positive reinforcement if he remains calm. Remember...if your car rides always end at the vet's office, your Akita may create negative associations with all car rides. To combat this, take him on rides that also stop at his favorite places, such as a park or a friend's house.

Be sure to equip your car so your dog has a comfortable ride. You may want to use a seat protector, a sheet, or towels to keep your backseat free of dog messes. Keep a bottle of cold water and a portable dog dish handy, so you can give your dog water whenever you make a stop. A favorite toy or chew bone can also comfort or entertain your dog during long rides. Since Akitas can easily

FUN FACT
The Ugly-Cute Akita

Wasao, an Akita dog living in Japan, became an internet sensation because of his unique looks, after being abandoned as a puppy in the town of Ajigasawa and adopted in 2007. His nickname was "busa kawaii," a combination of two Japanese words, "busaiku" meaning ugly, and "kawaii" meaning cute. Wasao passed away at the old age of 13 in June 2020.

overheat, be sure to direct the air conditioning toward your dog, or you can crack the windows, so he gets plenty of airflow.

If you are taking a long drive, you should take plenty of rests in safe places along the way. Some dogs are frightened by lots of traffic so find a spot where there are not a lot of cars nearby. You may want to keep your dog inside the car when you stop for gas, especially in a busy city, so the sound of traffic does not affect him, and so you are also able to keep your eye on him.

Before your trip, map out a few stops along the way that have a dog park or large rest stop, so you can give your dog plenty of exercise. By letting your dog stretch his legs and go to the bathroom somewhere safe, you are also creating a trip that is relaxing and stress-free for both you and your Akita.

Photo Courtesy of Dejahn Renrick

Photo Courtesy
of Jessica DeLucia

Flying and Hotel Stays

"I left my boy Hunter in the hotel room to go down the hall and get ice. I could hear him messing with the door handle in the room, which he had to pull down and pull towards him to be able to get out. The next thing I knew here he comes running down the hallway. They are super smart and you should never underestimate them."

CAROL FRIEDMAN
Sovereign Akitas

If you are traveling further from home, you might have to fly to your destination or to stay in a hotel along the way. Both situations can be especially tough on a dog. Akitas are not small dogs, so unless your dog is still a puppy, your adult Akita will likely not be allowed in the cabin of the airplane. Most airlines have rules that allow small dogs to ride in the cabin if they can fit under the seat as a carry-on bag would.

Larger dogs are usually forced to ride in the cargo hold in a secure crate. This can be a scary experience for a lot of dogs! The airplane is loud, the temperature is not as well-regulated as it is in the cabin, and the change in air pressure can be extremely uncomfortable. Also, Akitas tend to stick close to their owner, so your dog might not enjoy being away from you during a lengthy flight. So, before you leave, decide if the method of travel will create unwanted stress for your dog, or if it is even worth taking him along?

In situations where you cannot avoid flying with your dog, make sure to take the proper precautions to ensure your dog arrives safely at your destination. When you book the flight, check with the airline to make sure you can bring your dog along. Secure the contact information for the airline you are flying into; in case your dog is lost in transit, you night need to connect with the airline upon arrival. Some airlines may also require vaccination records, so ask the airline if there is any special documentation that you need to provide.

Equip your Akita's crate with a favorite blanket, a safe, comforting toy, and water. In case of a baggage handling mix-up, put up-to-date ID tags on your dog's collar, update your microchip information, and write your contact information on the crate. Before your flight, make sure your dog has had plenty of exercise and has gone to the bathroom. Many airport terminals now have dog areas where your Akita can relieve himself before take-off. If you have a layover in a different city, talk with the airline about where you can pick up your dog when you reach your final destination.

Photo Courtesy
of T&J Jennings
@Makana_Bear and @Panzie_Bear on IG

If you are staying in a hotel, you will want to take similar precautions to ensure your dog is safe and comfortable in a strange place. Many hotels do not allow dogs, or they charge extra fees; make sure you have confirmation beforehand that your Akita is allowed on the premises. It is not worth sneaking your dog into your room and to end up paying exorbitant fines when you are caught; or even worse, being kicked out of your room.

Try to book a hotel in an area with green space nearby, such as a park or open field. A hotel in the middle of a busy city may be overwhelming to your Akita, and it can make it difficult for your dog to get the exercise he needs.

During your hotel stay, keep your Akita as occupied as possible when in your room. A bored dog can become destructive, which could also be extremely costly if your dog destroys hotel property. To keep this from happening, keep plenty of toys on hand, so your dog can play or chew to relieve stress and to entertain himself.

Try to avoid leaving your Akita alone in your hotel room for extended periods of time. If you have to leave your dog for more than a couple of hours, consider taking him to a doggy daycare for the day. If you are staying at a hotel where you know you will not be able to spend a lot of time with your dog, consider leaving him at home. With the right arrangements, he will likely be happier under the supervision of a trusted caregiver than alone in a strange place.

Kenneling vs. Dog Sitters

If you cannot take your dog on your travels, do some research on kennels and dog sitters in your area. There are benefits and drawbacks to each, so choose the option that will be best for your Akita.

Kennels are generally the more affordable option because someone is taking care of multiple dogs at once, which means a group rate will be less expensive. If your Akita plays well with others, he may have fun interacting with other people and dogs at a kennel. However, since your dog will also be in close contact with other dogs, you will need to make sure your dog is current on his vaccinations.

Overnight kennels often have doggy daycares attached to their business, so you can take your dog to daycare before leaving on your trip. Staying in the daycare and becoming accustomed to the handlers and to being around other dogs will help your dog become comfortable with the kennel. This should make the transition from daycare to kennel much smoother.

Most kennels tend to have separate sleeping areas for dogs, so your dog will not always be in direct contact with other animals. Another major benefit of a kennel is knowing there will always be someone on staff to care for your dog. Some kennels even have a live video stream, so you can watch your pup and his activities from far away.

Before choosing a kennel, seek out recommendations from trusted dog owners. It will be much easier to leave your dog at home if you know he will be well taken care of.

On the other hand, if you know your Akita does not enjoy spending time around other dogs, consider hiring a dog sitter to care for him. A dog sitter is simply someone who will either watch your Akita in your home or in their home. Oftentimes, family and friends make good dog sitters because they know your dog – his likes, his dislikes, and his routine. However, the people close to you may not have the knowledge, time, or experience needed to take care of your Akita.

Professional dog sitters exist in virtually every city, and they usually come with references to share their past experiences and to help you feel comfortable leaving your pooch in their care. When vetting a dog sitter, make sure you speak to their references to gain more comfort regarding the sitter's abilities.

Regardless of your dog sitter, you will want to hire someone who can spend lots of time with your Akita, so he does not get lonely, bored, or anxious. A dog walker or someone who stops by the house a few times a day might not be enough to keep your Akita happy!

Tips and Tricks for Traveling

Traveling with an Akita can be difficult, so here are some tips that will help make your travels safe and smooth:

- Update all identification information before you go. If you have moved or changed phone numbers since getting your dog's tags or microchip, make a new tag and update the information with the microchip database. If you are leaving your dog with a sitter, leave information regarding your veterinary office – in case an emergency should arise.

- Create a travel bag dedicated strictly to your dog's travel supplies before the trip; by gathering things beforehand, you will be less likely to forget something the day of your trip. Fill the bag with food, treats, a bottle of water, portable dog dish, poop bags, toys, collars and harnesses, and any medications your dog will need.

- Ensure your dog has had plenty of exercise before and during your trip. A tired dog is easier to handle than a dog with lots of pent-up energy.

Go on a long walk before your drive or flight and take extra time to walk or play during every stop.

- Bring something familiar or soothing for your dog if you are traveling to an unfamiliar destination. An old blanket, chew toys, or even a white noise machine can be soothing for a worried pup when he is experiencing new sights, smells, and sounds.

- If your Akita is prone to anxiety, talk to your vet beforehand about medication or herbal supplements. They may provide you with something your dog can temporarily take to stay calm while traveling.

- Reinforce calm behavior in your dog with tasty treats. Traveling to a new place can be a learning experience so make it a positive one with lots of positive reinforcement.

- Before you leave, plan the stops you will make on the trip. If you are driving, map out a few safe places to stop where you can let your dog stretch his legs. A large rest stop may be a good place for a walk but without sacrificing too much of your travel time. A dog park in town is a safe spot to let your dog run without worrying about highway traffic. If you are flying, get to know your airport terminal by reading online maps and figure out where you can let your dog relieve himself - without missing your flight!

- Control your stress levels! Traveling can be stressful, even without traveling with a dog. Your dog will have a more positive experience if you are not giving off anxious energy, too. Plan ahead and give yourself extra time so your dog is not feeding off of your negativity!

CHAPTER 12

Nutrition

In order to look and feel his best, your Akita will need a healthy, balanced diet. With so many foods on the market, it can be challenging to pick the right one. Plus, it is hard to know what people foods you can and cannot feed your dog. This chapter will guide you through your dog's nutritional needs.

Photo Courtesy of Marshall Wolff

Importance of a Good Diet

A dog's diet is what fuels his body. The right nutrients can give your dog long-lasting energy to do the activities he loves. The right food can also keep his organs, bones, and muscles in good condition, leading to a long, healthy life. Good nutrition can even enhance your Akita's appearance because oils are what keeps a dog's coat shiny. If your dog does not eat the right kind or amount of food, he will gain or lose too much weight and will not feel well enough to play.

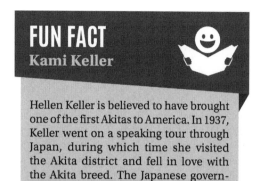

FUN FACT
Kami Keller

Hellen Keller is believed to have brought one of the first Akitas to America. In 1937, Keller went on a speaking tour through Japan, during which time she visited the Akita district and fell in love with the Akita breed. The Japanese government asked an Akita police officer who bred Akitas to give Keller a puppy. The puppy was named Kamikaze-Go and nicknamed "Kami." Unfortunately, Kami didn't live to see his first birthday and died of distemper at eight months old.

There are three basic macronutrients to include in your dog's diet. Carbohydrates supply your Akita with energy that he burns during exercise and play. In many commercial dog foods, this comes in the form of corn, wheat, or soy. Most dogs can digest these grains without issue, but some dogs are sensitive to them. Other good carbs to look for include potatoes, oatmeal, rice, and barley. Akitas are large dogs, so a majority of their food should be carbohydrates.

Proteins also provide energy, but they primarily help your dog stay strong and lean. Most dog foods contain chicken meal, which sounds unappetizing, but is perfectly healthy for dogs. Red meat sources, like beef, contain iron that supports healthy blood cells. Fish are also great for dogs because they contain fatty acids that support brain health and that keep your dog's coat shiny.

Fats are also a necessary part of your dog's diet. Fats provide long-lasting energy, support various bodily functions, and keep your dog's coat sleek and moisturized.

Finally, your dog's diet should include a good mix of vitamins and minerals. Virtually all commercial dog food brands contain a multivitamin supplement, but some formulas go above and beyond and contain real fruits and vegetables plus probiotics that support gut health.

If your Akita does not receive the correct nutrients, he may become overweight or underweight. Nutrient deficiencies can cause illnesses that shorten the life of your dog. Deficiencies will also cause your dog to appear lethargic or uninterested in the things he is used to doing. A lack of fats and oils in his diet might make his skin itchy and his fur dull and lackluster. Some dogs might develop an intolerance to certain dog food ingredients, which can cause digestive upset or an allergic reaction.

If you think your dog has a nutrient deficiency, or if his food does not appear to be satisfying his needs, talk to your vet about an alternative diet. Healthy food and plenty of exercise will make your dog happy and healthy; it will help him live a long, full life!

Photo Courtesy of Adia Robinson

Choosing a Commercial Dog Food

When shopping for your dog in the pet store, you will find several aisles devoted to dog food. The entire process can be overwhelming if you do not know what you are looking for!

When choosing a dog food, first pick food for the appropriate life stage of your dog. Puppy food is especially formulated to give pups the nutrients they need to develop, without causing them to grow too big too quickly. Adult food is the most common type of commercial dog food at the pet store and is what you will feed your dog once he is full-sized. As your dog enters his senior years, you may want to switch to a senior formula that has fewer calories and contains nutrients that support an aging dog's brain and joints.

You will also notice there are both wet and dry foods available. Wet foods are good if your dog has mouth problems that prohibit him from eating crunchy food. Oftentimes, older dogs have painful, decaying teeth, so their owners will switch to a wet food diet because eating is otherwise too painful for their Akita. Or, if a dog has other issues that keep him from eating, wet food or wet food mixed with dry food will produce a stronger aroma that will entice him to eat.

If your dog does not have any problems eating, a dry food is best. When a dog eats dry kibble, the food scrapes plaque off of his teeth as he eats. In contrast, wet food sticks to the teeth, which can lead to dental issues.

Along with regular brushing, feeding your dog dry food will improve his oral hygiene as well as keep him healthy.

Finally, you will notice a significant difference in price between the various brands of dog food on the market. The cheapest brands tend to contain cheap ingredients and inferior fillers. These satiate your dog, but they do not satisfy your dog's nutritional needs. The mid-priced foods have less fillers but can stay affordable to the consumer because they include animal and agricultural by-products that are not labeled for human consumption. This is not necessarily a bad thing, as fats, organ meats, and cartilage are all great for your dog's health. The most expensive dog food brands boast "natural" ingredients, but these come at a premium price that can be unaffordable for many owners. A middle-range dog food is fine for most dogs. Some brands promote a "grain-free" formula as a healthy alternative, but studies have shown these formulas can have a negative effect on your dog's heart health.

The first time you buy food for your Akita, you may want to buy what your breeder or the shelter previously fed your dog because some pups experience stomach upset when switching to a new food. If you want to switch formulas later on, combine the new and old food for a few days until your dog adjusts to the difference. Some dogs can be picky about their dog food flavors, so you might want to buy small bags of food until you are sure your dog loves the taste of the new brand.

If your dog experiences any digestive symptoms, talk to your vet about finding a new formula. There are lots of different dog foods that contain many different ingredients, so you might go through trial and error before you find the perfect food for your dog.

Cooking for Your Akita

Some dog owners prefer to make their own dog food instead of buying commercial brands because they want to provide strictly high-quality foods for their dogs. While this is an acceptable way to feed your Akita, it takes extra time, money, and knowledge of your Akita's nutritional needs to make this work.

Before starting your dog on a homemade diet, talk to your vet to be sure your Akita is a good candidate for this type of diet; plus, your vet may also show you recipes that will work well for your Akita. It can be dangerous to feed your dog a homemade diet without doing your research, so also talk with nutritional experts before starting out. Your recipe may cover a lot of essential vitamins and minerals from whole foods, but you will likely need a multivitamin supplement to ensure all bases are covered.

You will also need to keep a fresh supply of proteins on hand in order to offer the best quality of food to your dog. To give your dog a variety of fresh nutrients, try different meats. For example, chicken, beef, and fish will keep things interesting and will give your dog a variety of nutrients at the same time. Do not shy away from organ meats either because they are highly nutritious and dogs love the taste! If you are lucky, you may even be able to buy these straight from a local butcher, who may otherwise not use these cuts.

Vegetarian or vegan owners may be interested in feeding their dog a plant-based diet, but this method is not advised. Dogs and humans have different nutritional needs, so even if you do not eat meat, your dog should... you should always include meat in his diet.

Unlike humans, dogs can digest some raw meats without becoming sick, and they may even prefer their protein sources raw. However, you should always make sure you use fresh ingredients and to make sure your dog eats immediately after his food is served; this will reduce the chance of your dog being affected by a foodborne illness.

Carbs can come from vegetables or grains, such as sweet potatoes, barley, or brown rice.

Grain-free dog diets are trendy, but they can lead to heart disease. If your dog cannot tolerate certain grains, try different ingredients until you find a carb that your dog can digest. Some dogs have an intolerance to certain foods, but this does not mean an owner should cut out all carbohydrates.

Fruits and vegetables are also great for a dog's diet so try a variety with your dog to see which he enjoys. Homemade dog food is definitely not for every Akita or Akita owner; make sure you double-check with a vet before proceeding with this type of diet.

Photo Courtesy of Sophie Emma Windham

Feeding Table Scraps

It can be incredibly hard to resist those big Akita eyes as they gaze up at you and practically beg for a table scrap! Plus, many dog owners grew up in households where it was normal to give table scraps to the dog as a way of not wasting food. However, feeding your Akita "people food" can cause a myriad of health and behavioral issues for your dog.

For starters, dog food is meant to cover all nutritional needs; that is why feeding guides on the back of dog food bags are calculated to show the precise number of calories your dog needs. When you give your dog extra food from the table, you may be giving him more daily calories than he can burn, which will result in him becoming overweight.

Oftentimes, your human dinner might contain ingredients that are not good for your dog. For example, onions can make a dog extremely ill and are found in a lot of dishes. Also, giving your dog excess fat - many households cut the gristle off of their meats and give them to their dogs - can cause diseases in a dog. Cooked bones splinter easily and can get caught in a dog's digestive tract. Why would you risk all these health problems when your dog can receive the correct balance of nutrients by simply choosing the right dog food for him?

Behavioral issues can also arise if you give your dog table scraps. Food is a powerful reward, so if you give him food from the table, you will reinforce the habit of begging for food. He may also start sitting and whining near the table during dinnertime, and he might even try to snatch food off the table. He will quickly learn to associate your dinnertime with his reward and will pester you until you give him a treat. This can be annoying to deal with, but it can also potentially lead to your dog getting sick if he gets into the habit of taking food off the table or running to gobble food dropped on the floor.

This does not mean you cannot give any table food to your dog. The right types of human food can make excellent treats, but what and how you feed your dog will make a significant difference.

Foods like chocolate, onions, grapes, avocados, meat scraps with excessive fat, or cooked bones should definitely be off-limits! Chocolate, onions, and grapes can all cause serious injuries to internal organs and to blood cells when eaten in small quantities. Avocado pits can be a choking hazard and can obstruct the digestive system if swallowed. Excessive fat is not good for your dog's internal organs, especially the pancreas. Plus, while raw bones can make fine chew toys, cooked bones can splinter and become lodged in your dog's mouth or digestive tract. If you want to know more about dangerous foods, the ASPCA's website has valuable information regarding people foods, plants, and household products that should be avoided.

Foods that are acceptable for your dog are sweet potatoes or blueberries, which also provide excellent nutrition. Small bits of hot dogs or canned tuna can make fantastic training treats because of their strong smell. You may drop a piece of fruit in your dog's dish as a special treat or use a cooked carrot to reward your dog for sitting on command during your regular training time. However, when giving your dog people food, make sure it is not around your dinner table or during a family meal!

Treats

There are so many types of commercial dog treats on the market, it can be hard to choose the right ones to buy. If you want to motivate your dog, your best bet is to buy treats that contain some moisture. Jerky strips or soft chews smell appetizing to dogs because of the moisture content. However, if you are using a lot of treats during training, you will also want to be mindful of the calories you are adding to your dog's diet.

Dog food feeding recommendations do not take extra treats into account. If you give your dog a whole jerky strip or biscuit every time he completes a command, you will be adding excessive calories to his diet! If he eats too many treats, he might have digestive upset or refuse to eat his dog food. Instead, buy training treats that are small and have a low-calorie count. Another option is to take larger treats and break them into small pieces before training.

In the beginning, buy a few treats in assorted flavors to see which ones your dog likes best or use one flavor and periodically switch to a new one to keep him interested. You will see the best results in your training when you have a powerful reward – one your dog loves!

Weight Management

Akitas, like every dog, can put on extra weight if they are eating more calories than they are burning. Excess weight can be a problem for your Akita because it puts stress on your dog's skeletal system and makes it harder for his organs to function properly.

Weight gain is primarily caused by overfeeding. Your dog's daily food recommendation should not be exceeded, even if he gobbles his food quickly. The amount of food he should eat a day is carefully calculated by dog food companies, so it is important to use the weight guide on the bag.

Remember, treats factor into the daily calorie count, so if your Akita starts packing on the pounds and you are not sure why, calculate how many calories he receives from treats and include that information with his daily caloric intake.

Since Akitas are such a fluffy animal, it can be hard to even notice if yours is gaining weight! Perhaps the best way to tell if your dog has a healthy shape is by looking at your dog from above after he has taken a bath. A healthy body should have a clear tuck at the waist, just before his hips. If his sides are straight (or round) from his shoulders to his hips, he may have excess body fat. You should also be able to feel his ribs but not see them.

If you have any concern about your dog gaining weight, talk to your vet. At every visit, your vet will weigh your dog; this will enable you to compare any changes in your dog's body from year to year. Plus, your vet can advise you of any medical conditions that might lead to your Akita's weight gain.

If your dog is overweight, start adjusting his diet immediately. If he is eating too many high-calorie treats, switch to low-cal treats when you are training him. Make sure you are not overfeeding your dog with his regular meals and slowly cut back on the amount of food you give him. You can also increase your dog's exercise if he has become a couch potato but be sure you do not overdo it. Extra exercise can be hard on a dog that has become out of shape. Akitas are prone to heat exhaustion so take it easy on the exercise. Go on longer walks in the morning or evening when it is cooler or spend a few extra minutes playing.

If a slight reduction in food and extra exercise is not cutting it, talk to your vet about switching to a weight-loss dog food. The best way to keep your dog in good shape is to avoid overfeeding and to ensure he is getting his recommended amount of exercise every day.

CHAPTER 13
Grooming Your Akita

Akitas are beautiful dogs with soft, thick coats, so grooming is obviously a necessary part of this dog's daily care. Without proper grooming, your Akita can develop painful mats of hair and irritating skin conditions. Plus, grooming is more than just brushing your dog's fur; clean teeth, trimmed toenails, and heathy eyes and ears are included, which can improve the overall health and wellbeing of your dog. This chapter will give you tips on how to groom your dog at home.

Photo Courtesy of Elly Rodgers

Coat Basics

The Akita is a double-coated dog, which means they have a sleek topcoat and a fluffy undercoat. This coat type is perfect for temperature regulation of their body; in other words, it keeps your dog warm in the winter and cool in the summer.

However, this type of coat also takes more maintenance than with most dogs. Even if the coat looks smooth and tangle-free on the top, there could be small mats and tangles underneath that might only get worse if your dog is not brushed regularly. Additionally, dead skin cells or moisture can get trapped underneath a matted coat, which will cause irritation to your dog's skin.

Regular brushing can remove loose fur, exfoliate dry skin, and remove any dirt in your dog's coat, making your dog happy and much more comfortable! However, be aware of overbathing your pup because this can be hard on your dog's skin and fur due to stripping necessary oils from his coat. Dogs only need a bath once every three to four months - unless they get particularly dirty. Otherwise, most dirt and debris can be brushed off or wiped out with a damp cloth.

Managing Your Akita's Coat Blow

"The Akita has a thick double coat which will shed twice a year. The only way to remove the undercoat is with a high powered blower. They must be used to standing on a grooming table because this process takes several hours. I recommend that you take them to a groomer have them blow all the hair out during these shedding times twice a year and be done with it."

CAROL FRIEDMAN
Sovereign Akitas

Twice a year, you will notice your Akita is shedding much more than usual. This seasonal shedding is referred to as a dog "blowing his coat." In the spring and fall, your Akita will lose his undercoat in large tufts. This occurs because your dog is preparing his undercoat to protect him in the winter or summer months. Coat blowing can be a very messy process, but it can be managed with proper grooming. Unfortunately, the frequent vacuuming during this time of year is hard to avoid!

Using a variety of brushes will help you tackle the coat blowing process. This two-part process begins with a basic pin brush, which will grab hold of the loose fur and pull it from the rest of the coat.

Once you have removed as much loose fur as possible with the pin brush, switch to a slicker brush. Bristles on this brush are thinner and can help break up any mats that have developed. The blowing the coat process will detangle and remove loose fur that is trapped close to the skin. If your Akita is especially tangled, a rake brush will break up the tougher knots. You can also purchase specialty brushes for this process at pet stores, which are designed to remove a ton of loose fur. However, a few basic brushes and some patience will most likely do the trick.

Rest assured these shedding seasons do not last forever! Yet, it can be hard to deal with when your Akita leaves fluffy balls of fur wherever he goes. One way to reduce the mess is to set aside time to brush your Akita outside on a daily basis. This tactic prevents a majority of the fur from ever entering the house. You may also want to cover your dog's favorite spots with old bedding or towels that can easily be washed to remove the excess hair. In the meantime, you will simply have to resign yourself to the fact your vacuum cleaner and your lint roller will be getting a good workout!

Bath Time

You will definitely know when it is bath time for your Akita due to the fact that he does not smell quite as fresh as usual! You should always make sure you have the right supplies before even starting the bath water.

First, choose a shampoo that is specifically made for dogs, as a dog's skin and coat require different cleaning ingredients than what is in shampoo for humans.

There are many different dog shampoos on the market, so a gentle formula made for sensitive skin is probably a safe bet. Dogs can be sensitive to strong scents, so a lightly scented product (or fragrance-free) will also be important. Having a detachable showerhead is helpful when you have to quickly rinse your dog instead of having to pour cups of water on him to get him clean. You will want a washcloth and some old towels on hand to gently clean your dog's face and to dry him once the job is finished.

Make sure the water is a comfortable temperature before putting your pup in the tub. An uncomfortable first-bathing experience can make it harder to bathe your dog in the future. Use water that is warm but not too hot. After your dog is completely soaked, lather shampoo all over his coat, avoiding anything above his neck. After a good scrub, rinse your Akita very thoroughly. Excess shampoo residue can cause your dog to feel itchy and can make his coat dull.

Next, take a damp cloth; carefully and gently wipe your dog's face, keeping all water from getting into his eyes and ears. You can wipe your dog's outer ear with a warm cloth, but do not allow excess moisture into his ear canal because this can promote an ear infection. Once your dog is clean, take him out of the tub, dry him, and let him shake out the rest of the water on his own.

Some dogs do not like baths, which can make the bathing pro-cess unpleasant for both dog and owner. One way to help your dog feel

comfortable is to control any feelings of frustration when you are wrestling an upset dog into the tub. Stay calm, talk to your dog in a soothing voice, and be mindful of actions that may upset your dog, such as suddenly spraying him with the hose.

Another way to make the bathing process more positive is to give your Akita plenty of treats. Once he is in the tub, give him a treat and tell him he is being a good dog. Before you take him out of the tub, give him another treat. Finally, give him one more treat once he is out of the water and dried off. This type of positive reinforcement can show your dog that baths do not have to be a negative experience!

Trimming Toenails

Trimming your Akita's toenails can be a nerve-wracking experience, but it is something that is necessary for your dog's health and for his comfort. Overgrown nails can scratch and split, and they can also put uncomfortable pressure on your dog's feet. Nails that are too long can even lead to arthritis because of the extra pressure on foot and ankle joints. In order to keep your dog's paws happy, trim his nails whenever they are long enough to touch the floor when he stands.

There are different trimming tools on the market for accomplishing this task. Basic clippers work well for most owners, though it takes some time to figure out how to cut nails to the correct length without cutting them too short. Or there are grinding tools that slowly sand your dog's nail to a blunt edge. These grinding tools cannot remove an overgrown toenail quickly, but they are good for routine maintenance.

The important thing to be aware of when cutting a dog's toenails is that cutting too far into the nail can be very painful. The "quick" is the blood supply to the nail that can bleed a lot when nicked and is located at the end of the nail that meets the skin on the paw. If you accidentally cut into the quick, the experience will be very painful and somewhat traumatizing to your dog, which will only make the chore more difficult in the future. If your Akita has white nails, the pink quick is visible. In black nails, it can be hard to tell where the quick starts. So, it is best to clip small pieces of the nail until it is at the right length - just barely off the floor when your dog is standing. If you can hear nails clicking on the floor when he walks, they are too long and need to be cut!

If you cut the quick of your dog's nails, try not to panic, or your dog will become even more upset. If you have styptic powder on hand, which can be found at pet stores, put some on the cut nail to stop the bleeding. If you do not have styptic powder at home, you can use cornstarch as an alternative; just dip the nail in the powder and apply pressure. You might also need to hold a clean cloth against your dog's nail for up to a half hour to get the bleeding to stop. Once the bleeding is controlled, you may want to find something to cover your dog's paw to prevent blood from getting on your carpet or furniture - a sock works just fine.

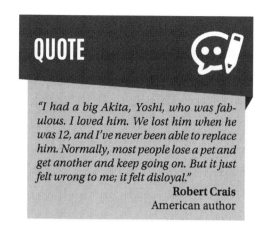

QUOTE

"I had a big Akita, Yoshi, who was fabulous. I loved him. We lost him when he was 12, and I've never been able to replace him. Normally, most people lose a pet and get another and keep going on. But it just felt wrong to me; it felt disloyal."
Robert Crais
American author

Many dogs do not like having their nails cut even if they have never experienced a nail being cut to the quick. This fear might stem from a dislike of having their paws touched. However, to set up your dog for nail-trimming success, practice touching your dog's paws and nails before introducing the nail clipper. If your dog stays calm while you touch his paws, reward and praise him. As your dog is more comfortable with his paws being touched, introduce the clipper or nail grinder and let him sniff them out. Place the tools near his toenails and reward him if he is calm. After a time, your dog will be less startled by the clippers and having his paws touched and will make a smooth transition when you trim his nails.

Brushing Teeth

Good dental fitness is also an essential part of your dog's overall health and wellbeing. Not only does brushing keep your dog's breath fresh and his teeth sparkly, but it can potentially extend your dog's life by keeping tooth decay bacteria from spreading to other parts of the body. Plus, tooth decay and gum disease can be extremely uncomfortable for a dog, so frequent cleaning can also prevent these issues.

Before brushing your dog's teeth for the first time, you will need to purchase a small toothbrush that will fit in your dog's mouth. Pet stores sell different types of dog toothbrushes. Some look like small versions of traditional toothbrushes, and others are silicon brushes that fit over your index finger. The latter style of brush might be easier to use. You will also need dog toothpaste, chicken or peanut butter flavor, which are appetizing to a dog. These toothpastes are also safe if your dog accidentally swallows the paste.

Before you use the toothbrush, make sure your Akita is comfortable with you touching his teeth. Try putting a little toothpaste on your finger and letting your dog him lick the toothpaste off. This will let him experience the taste of the toothpaste without the strange sensation of brushing.

Next, gently lift up your dog's lips and examine his teeth. If he is comfortable with this action, gently touch the outside of his canines. When your Akita is comfortable with you looking at his teeth, lift up his lips and brush them with the toothbrush. Brush one side of his mouth, then give him a short break before moving onto the other side. If you brush his teeth on a daily basis, you may be able to prolong your dog's professional dental cleanings or avoid them altogether.

If you take your Akita to the veterinarian to have his teeth cleaned, you need to now the professional cleaning process can be hard on a dog and expensive for the owner. Vets must sedate the dog before cleaning his teeth, and Akitas tend to be hard to sedate, which means this process could be long and involved plus potentially dangerous for your dog. This information alone should act as incentive to brush your dog's teeth on a regular basis. Not only will good oral hygiene keep your Akita from getting doggy breath, but it will improve his overall health, too.

Cleaning Ears and Eyes

If your Akita's ears or eyes become dirty, each might be susceptible to infection. Even though this is a necessary part of your dog's grooming, it is important to be careful when cleaning around these sensitive areas. When your pup's ears get dirty or hold excess moisture, they can become smelly, inflamed, and infected, which can be very painful for your dog.

One way to prevent ear problems is to keep your dog's ears free of water when bathing him. If your dog plays in the rain or goes swimming, wipe the outer parts of the ear and allow your dog to shake the water out when he is finished.

If your Akita has waxy residue in his ears and is scratching his ears often, try cleaning them with a cleaning solution sold at pet stores. This solution will break up ear wax, which your dog will shake out of the inner ear when he shakes his head. Squirt the cleaner in his ear, then rub the outer base of the ear for a few seconds to work the solution into the ear canal; let him shake out the solution. If residue collects on the outer part of the ear, wipe it with a cloth moistened in ear cleaner. However, never touch the inner part of your dog's ears, especially with a small object like a cotton swab.

Eyes generally do not take a lot of cleaning, but you may notice dried tears in the corners of your dog's eyes. This can easily be cleaned by gently wiping your dog's eyes with a warm, damp cloth. Akitas have short hair on their faces, so long fur in the eyes should not be a problem. If you ever notice that your Akita's eyes are red and have gooey discharge or they have more tears than usual, consult your veterinarian, as this could be a sign of an eye infection.

CHAPTER 14
Basic Health Care

Your Akita's health care is extremely important, but it can easily be forgotten when mixed with the demands of every-day life. However, preventative care is key to your dog's good health and can save you time and money if you follow the routine your veterinarian creates for your Akita. This chapter will walk you through some of the basics of your Akita's health care, so your dog can live a long and healthy life.

Fleas and Ticks

"Akitas are sensitive to vaccine and chemicals in the flea and tick medications. I don't advise the combination pills as it's too much for their system. I prefer Advantix K9 to topical and the individual heart guard for heart worms but not given at the same time."

CAROL FRIEDMAN
Sovereign Akitas

Photo Courtesy
of Angel Allen Martin

Fleas and ticks are both external parasites that feed on your Akita's blood. These bugs attach to your Akita after he has been playing outside, especially in tall grass, or playing with other animals. These parasites can carry disease and can cause anemia if too much blood has been lost. Luckily, these pests can be avoided by using a monthly topical or oral medication prescribed by a veterinarian.

Some oral medications are effective for several months, so you only have to remember to give your dog a pill a couple times a year. These medications work by either repelling the bug before it latches onto your dog's skin, or by killing the parasite once it has been ingested and is in your dog's blood. Veterinary clinics tend to have favorite pesticide products for this purpose, usually kept in stock, so talk to your vet about which products they recommend.

If your dog gets a tick stuck to his skin, be careful when removing it. Make sure to grasp the tick near the head and gently pull the whole tick off. Otherwise, you risk ripping off the tick's body and leaving the head attached to your dog's skin, which can lead to infection. If you are concerned that the tick may be carrying a disease, you can place the whole tick in a bag and have your vet examine it.

If undetected and if your dog likes to hop in your bed or on the couch with you, ticks can detach and find a human source of blood. Be cautious! Stop ticks from entering your home and finding a new host by always checking your dog after playing outdoors and before reentering the house.

Fleas are another pest that can be difficult to get rid of if your Akita becomes infested. These insects reproduce very quickly, and they can easily jump from place to place, making them hard to catch and to kill. If your dog has fleas, you will need to take care of the problem immediately before it spreads!

Bathe your Akita using flea shampoo; then, comb through his fur with a flea comb and crush any insect you find in his fur. Flea shampoos can be purchased at pet stores and should only be used to treat an infestation, not as a preventative action. Carefully read the directions to make sure you are using the medicated formula effectively and appropriately.

Once your dog is clean, you will have to thoroughly clean your home, or your dog may become reinfested. Wash all bedding in hot water if your dog has used it and vacuum every surface of your home. Fleas can lay eggs in the tiny cracks in your floorboards or nooks in your couch and return in no time.

If you still cannot shake the flea problem, purchase a flea-killing cleaning spray that will kill eggs, or you can use a bug bomb in all affected areas. With enough diligence, you will be able to rid your dog and home of fleas... do not give up!

If your current flea prevention program is not working, see your veterinarian about a more effective preventative treatment. Avoid flea collars, especially if you own cats, because they can make cats extremely sick and may not be the healthiest flea and tick prevention for dogs either.

Photo Courtesy
of Elfi Bonn

Worms and Internal Parasites

Internal parasites are another type of creature that can make your dog extremely ill. Internal parasites include different types of worms that attack vital organs and steal nutrients by feeding on your dog's blood. When worms are feeding on your Akita, he will not get the nutrients he needs to remain healthy.

Intestinal worms are somewhat common in dogs - especially in puppies. Some puppies are even born with worms because they become infected through their mothers. Contaminated soil, other small animals, and animal feces are also common sources of worms. Dogs love to eat things they shouldn't, so it is not hard for a dog to pick up an intestinal parasite. Luckily, these parasites can be treated fairly easily.

If you find worms in your dog's stool, your vet will want a sample, so he can prescribe the proper medication to eliminate the problem. These infestations tend to clear up quickly, but you need to be aware of their possibility; your dog might have worms, and you might not even realize it.

If you see your Akita is looking lethargic, has abnormal bowel movements, or appears generally under the weather, you might need to collect a stool sample for your vet to analyze. Other common symptoms of worms are diarrhea, bloating, weight loss, blood in stool, and vomiting. If your dog has persistent diarrhea or vomiting, you should take your dog to the vet to be examined. More serious symptoms, like bloody stool, should warrant an immediate call to your vet's office.

Hookworms, whipworms, tapeworms, and roundworms are also common types of intestinal worms, but only roundworms and tapeworms can be seen with the naked eye.

Roundworms are the most common type of intestinal worms, especially in puppies because they can be spread from mother to pup. If you see a long, thin worm that does not have segments in your dog's stool, it may be a roundworm.

Tapeworms can latch onto dogs if they eat fleas that are infested with tapeworm eggs. Tapeworms are visible to the naked eye, so you may find segments of tapeworm in your dog's stool. If your dog displays any stomach issues that do not clear up after a few hours, you will need to prepare a stool sample to take to your vet. Your vet can analyze the stool sample through laboratory tests to determine the cause of discomfort. Since tapeworms can be transmitted through ingesting fleas, this is another reason to stay up to date on your dog's flea and tick prevention.

Hookworms are intestinal worms that can cause anemia in dogs, due to blood loss. Fatigue is a common symptom of anemia, so if your dog shows intestinal discomfort and appears lethargic, he may have hookworms.

Whipworms live in the large intestine and their eggs can survive outside of a host in a warm and moist environment for years. Animal feces and deceased animals can host these worms and eggs, so it is important to keep your yard clean and to avoid these nuisances when going for a walk.

Fortunately, de-worming medication, along with a bland diet, will help your dog return to normal. In some cases, a dog may need to take several rounds of de-worming medication, but the problems should clear up before long. A word of caution...if an infestation of intestinal worms is not treated when first noticed, your dog can become extremely ill and can cause death, especially in puppies.

Heartworms are another parasite that feeds off a dog's internal organs, and they can be deadly if not caught in time. When a dog is bitten by a mosquito that carries the heartworm parasite, the worms enter the dog's body through the bloodstream, moves through the blood vessels, and takes up residence in a dog's heart. The condition is treatable when caught early, but it can cause serious illness and even death if treated too late.

Luckily, your Akita can take a preventative pill each month to protect him from this dangerous parasite. Plus, these pills come in tasty flavors with a treat-like texture, so in this situation, your dog will be happy to take their meds.

Your vet will likely test your dog's blood for heartworms periodically; usually on a yearly basis as he prescribes a six month or year-long supply of the heartworm medicine. Not all veterinarians test for heartworms on an annual basis, so you need to be proactive and discuss this with your dog's vet.

If your vet suspects that your dog has heartworms, they may need to do additional testing, including ultrasounds or echocardiograms. Heartworms can be scary, but if you can remember to give your dog a pill once a month, you won't have to worry about it.

Photo Courtesy of Adriana Balas

Supplements and Natural Health Care

Natural health care and supplements can be controversial among dog owners and canine experts. Some dog owners prefer to use "natural" methods of keeping their dog healthy, as opposed to using traditional veterinary care and pharmaceuticals. This type of health care usually relies on supplements that contain herbs. There is some evidence that suggests certain herbs and naturally occurring ingredients might boost your dog's health.

For example, glucosamine, which is found in animal cartilage, is thought to be excellent for joint health in dogs. Fish oil is another common supplement that can keep a dog's skin moisturized and can give them a shiny coat if their diet lacks healthy fats and oils. Probiotics may help with a dog's digestive system, especially if he has a sensitive stomach and occasional diarrhea. Antioxidants are typically found in dog foods, but additional antioxidant supplements may fight signs of aging, such as cognitive decline and heart disease. Some herbal supplement blends on the market may help calm an anxious dog during thunderstorms or car rides, and they can be given when necessary, without a prescription.

If your dog does not respond to modern pain or anxiety treatments, acupuncture and acupressure are Eastern medicine alternatives for a dog. Acupuncture is the practice of placing small needles at certain pressure points along the body. Acupressure is a similar practice that uses pressure applied by hands instead of inserting needles. These are remedies that should be discussed with your dog's vet before taking your dog to a canine acupuncturist.

For an at-home fix for pain, you may try massage with your dog. Before starting out, see an animal massage expert for tips. Once you learn how to massage a dog for their specific needs, you can gently prepare an aging dog for a walk, aid in your dog's digestion, or soothe an anxious dog. Some of the touch therapies, such as massage or acupressure, that humans try when medication isn't enough may be effective on dogs as well.

When considering non-pharmaceutical remedies, consult with a veterinarian first. "Natural" does not always mean healthy, and consumers are often tricked into a false sense of safety because natural remedies seem harmless. Not only can some "natural" remedies be harmful, but they are often given in place of life saving pharmaceuticals that can improve a dog's life.

Every dog is different and not all supplements work well for all dogs. For example, some owners may swear by fish oil supplements, but your dog may get enough fat in his food, and extra fat might contribute to liver disease. Similarly, acupuncture may sound like a better alternative to pain medication, but your dog may suffer if the acupuncture is not working. Supplements or non-traditional medicine may improve your dog's health and give him a shiny coat, but they should not replace medicine prescribed by a vet.

Always talk to a vet before trying out a new treatment. Your vet has your dog's best interest in mind and will help you make the best decisions for your pet.

Vaccinations

Vaccinations are a necessary part of your dog's preventative health care, and they can also keep other dogs healthy, too. When you visit the vet for your Akita's yearly checkup, your vet will make sure your pup is up to date on his shots. Some vaccines are legally required, like rabies, but others are the owner's choice.

Also, many trainers and boarding facilities require all dogs supply records of their shots before they can enter. The more dogs that are vaccinated, the harder it is for a virus to spread, which could save the lives of many dogs. Remember, the cost of a vaccine pales in comparison to the stress a preventable illness puts on you and your dog.

If you visit the same vet office for every checkup, you will not need to worry about what shots your dog has had because their office will keep a detailed list of vaccine records. If you switch clinics, they will make sure you have your dog's records available to take to the new vet.

Most vets will give you a print-out of your dog's records after every visit, or they will refer you to an online database for current information. It is a good idea to have these records on hand, so you can tell your vet what services your dog needs.

Your dog will need shots for rabies, DHPP, and Bordetella. Additionally, there are other regional viruses, like Rocky Mountain Spotted Fever, which may require a different vaccine. Your vet will be sure to tell you which vaccinations your dog needs; all you need to do is bring your Akita to the clinic when they send you a reminder to schedule a visit!

CELEBRITY DOGS
Superdog
★★★★

Henry Cavill, best known for his lead roles in Superman and The Witcher, is a proud owner of an Akita. Cavill's pup, named Kal, loves to accompany the actor to the gym and on set. Fans of the actor and his dog can get a frequent glimpse of both on Cavill's Instagram (@henrycavill), where the duo have amassed 12 million followers.

Pet Insurance

Health insurance is no longer just for humans. You and your Akita can also benefit from an insurance policy, which can help if your dog suddenly has a major veterinary expense. Many veterinary clinics, especially larger chains, offer different kinds of health plans that can make veterinary care more affordable. They are usually in-house payment plans that offer options when paying a large vet bill if you are unable to cover things upfront.

Another option is to purchase pet insurance through a major insurance carrier. In fact, as pet ownership becomes more common, some employers are starting to offer pet insurance as a standard benefit to their employees. There are usually different types of policies to choose from - some will cover

Photo Courtesy of Suzye Landry

basic preventative care, like your Akita's regular checkups, while other plans will cover illness, injury, or chronic conditions. You will likely have to pay the full vet bill upfront after the first visit, but you will be reimbursed by your insurance carrier after filing a claim.

For the average Akita who lives a healthy life with few healthcare expenses, your monthly premiums will likely exceed what you will otherwise pay in vet bills. However, if your dog unexpectedly becomes sick or injured, pet insurance can save you money in the long run.

If you want to make sure you have plenty of funds to take care of your Akita and do not want to pay insurance for an otherwise healthy dog, you can always set aside money every month for your dog's healthcare needs. Veterinary care can be expensive, especially emergency care, so it is important to be prepared for any unexpected expense.

Genetic Health of Akitas

The average Akita will live a relatively healthy life with no major illnesses. However, there are some diseases that Akitas are more susceptible to than other dogs. Oftentimes, this is due to breeding because health conditions are bred along with physical and temperamental traits. An Akita that was bred by a reputable breeder should have fewer of these common conditions than Akitas bred by inexperienced breeders. Your Akita may never show any of these common genetic illnesses, but it is a good idea to be aware of these symptoms so your vet can diagnose and treat any medical concerns.

In terms of the skeletal system, some Akitas may have issues with their back legs because of how they are shaped. Cruciate ligament tears can occur if an Akita makes a sudden movement, such as jumping off a piece of furniture or turning a sharp corner. These types of injuries must be surgically repaired.

One way to prevent these potential injuries is to nip bad habits in the bud. When you catch your dog trying to jump from couch to couch, redirect their attention and give them praise when they stay on the floor.

Hip dysplasia is another common condition that occurs when the hip joint does not fit into the socket correctly. This can cause pain for a dog, especially in his older years. If left untreated, arthritis can become an issue. Since this is such a common concern among Akitas, most breeders screen their dogs for this condition. If you notice your dog is limping or cannot tolerate weight on one leg, your vet may be able to diagnose an injury or prescribe anti-inflammatory medication.

Akitas can also be more susceptible to different kinds of autoimmune disorders, such as hypothyroidism. Some of these autoimmune disorders affect skin and eyes, so if your dog's skin looks flaky, red, or inflamed, there may be an internal reason for the appearance of these symptoms. Other diseases will affect your dog's energy levels, so a once-peppy dog who is suddenly lethargic should be examined.

Autoimmune disorders can be diagnosed through blood tests. By explaining your dog's symptoms to your vet, they should be able to determine the right tests to run.

This breed may also develop eye problems, such as progressive renal atrophy or glaucoma. Both of these conditions can cause gradual blindness. If you notice that your dog's eyes look cloudy or are otherwise different than usual, a vet may be able to prescribe medication or treatment that can slow the loss of vision.

If your dog is going blind, you may not immediately notice because dogs are good at adapting to gradual vision loss. This problem might not surface until you notice your Akita is starting to bump into furniture after you rearrange a room. Nonetheless, an Akita with vision loss can still live a long and happy life.

Akitas are also somewhat prone to bloat, which is a scary condition involving the stomach. If the stomach is overfilled with gas, the stomach can twist, cutting off blood flow to the body. Dogs with bloat may retch, excessively salivate, have weakness or difficulty breathing, and appear uncomfortable. Overfeeding, overwatering, and too much physical activity after eating may cause bloat. Other digestive system ailments can also lead to a higher risk of bloat. If you suspect your dog has bloat, take him to an emergency vet because this condition requires immediate surgery.

If you are concerned about your dog suffering from bloat, you may try a slow-feeder bowl that has obstacles in the middle that keeps your dog from scarfing down his food. You should also feed your dog twice a day, instead of giving him one larger meal once a day. Keep your dog calm immediately after eating even if he wants to go to your backyard and run off his energy after dinner.

Finally, the things your dog ingests can have a significant impact on his health. When possible, help your dog avoid eating non-food items. This includes household objects left within reach, cleaning and lawn chemicals, or even people food. Additionally, you should watch what your dog eats outside of your home. When on a walk, it is easy for your Akita to sneak a bite of roadkill, poop, or trash found on the side of the road.

When playing outside, your dog may lap up water from stagnant puddles, streams, or other bodies of water. Parasites or toxic algae can make a dog extremely sick. When possible, carry fresh water while outside, so your dog has safe water to drink.

CHAPTER 15
Your Aging Akita

"If you can keep your senior dog active it really helps their mind and body. Mental stimulation is so good for them. Go for walks to keep their muscles active, it really helps with the aging process."

LINDA BACCO
Shogitai Akitas

Photo Courtesy
of Heidi Stone

Health care for your aging Akita can sometimes be more complicated than basic preventative care. When your Akita ages, you will want to cater toward his senior needs. This chapter will explain situations in which your Akita will need more specialized care and will discuss when it is time to make end-of-life decisions.

Caring for Your Aging Akita

Once your Akita is around seven or eight years old, he will be considered a senior dog. However, your Akita could live for another six to seven years in this senior phase. Senior dogs can continue to live a long and healthy life, but they will need extra care once they begin aging, as many years of play can be hard on a pup.

Initially, you may notice a change in your dog's metabolism because he is not looking as slim as usual. Senior dogs generally do not need as many calories as younger dogs because their body changes its caloric needs, and they are not as active as they once were.

Some vets recommend owners switch to a senior dog food formula to give their canines the nutrients they need without feeding them too many calories. This way, your dog will still feel full because he is eating the same quantity of food while consuming a smaller number of calories.

If you notice your senior dog gaining weight, gradually reduce daily meals and continue gentle exercise (like shorter walks) to see if the pounds come off. If not, talk to your vet about switching to a formula that keeps senior dogs from gaining too much extra fat.

Poor dental health and tooth loss is also common in advanced age. An old dog may have difficulty chewing crunchy kibble, especially with missing teeth. You may choose to switch to wet food or to mix small amounts of warm water with the dry food to soften it. Also, broth may add to the aroma and make the food more appetizing to a dog that is not interested in eating; however, make sure any human foods you add to your dog's food does not contain onion or excess salt.

With time, your older Akita may become slower and stiffer than when he was as a young dog. Joint supplements, like ones containing glucosamine, may help with pain. Prescription, anti-inflammatory meds from your vet can help on a short-term basis. However, these drugs may be hard on your dog's internal organs in the long term and are usually only prescribed when absolutely necessary.

Keep daily walks short and avoid long or rough games because arthritis is common in senior dogs, which can cause a lot of pain and discomfort.

Photo Courtesy of Alfredo Perez

Your dog may even benefit from a gentle warm-up or post-play massage to soothe sore muscles and joints.

If your dog likes water, aqua therapy can be a much gentler form of exercise than going on walks. Some veterinary facilities have warm pools with treadmills that allow dogs to get their steps without putting pressure on their joints. The warmth of the water can also be soothing. If no such facilities exist in your area, a swim in a clean lake or pond may provide therapeutic benefits and allow your dog to move around.

If you reduce your dog's physical exercise, it is still important to keep your senior dog mentally active. All dogs need entertainment to keep themselves from getting grouchy or depressed, but senior dogs can suffer from dementia if they do not receive mental stimulation.

Puzzle toys filled with treats can keep a senior dog entertained for a long time. If your dog's teeth are too damaged to chew on bones, your Akita will enjoy gently pushing levers on a puzzle board or licking peanut butter out of a rubber toy. You can even simply hide a treat in one of your closed fists and have your dog search for it.

Gentle games of catch can also keep your dog happy but make sure your senior dog does not have to run too fast or jump too high during the game, as this is when injury occurs.

You also may have to make changes to your home's layout for your dog. Senior dogs may lose some of the puppy fat that protects their bones and joints as they age, which can make them uncomfortable when they rest

Photo Courtesy of Ayden Smith

Photo Courtesy of Claudia van Dijk

on the hard floor. Make sure your dog has a cushioned, supportive bed. If your Akita frequently sits on the couch or lies on the bed with you, some steps or a small platform may make it easier for him to spend time with you.

Slippery floors may also cause a problem for older dogs, so a large rug on a hard floor can make your dog much more comfortable and keep him safer. You might also want to use a paw wax on your dog's pads to help them grip the hard floor better, or you can purchase foot coverings that give your dog more grip.

If your dog loses his vision, be sure to keep furniture away from walkways or from spaces where he is likely to run into them, and do not suddenly change the layout of your home.

Akitas sometimes experience blindness as they age, but this should not substantially affect your dog's quality of life. Dogs are good at adapting to their vision loss and can get around well as long as their routines and paths are not changed.

Hearing loss can also change the way you interact with your Akita, but it will not hurt his overall quality of life either. It can be frustrating to call your dog and to watch him ignore you. However, you can rely on the fact that he will still read your nonverbal cues if his vision is intact. If you used visual commands to accompany your verbal commands during obedience training, he will understand your command even though he may not hear you.

If your Akita used to walk without a leash, you will want to use one now if he starts losing his sense of sight or hearing. A leash will help keep him safe when he cannot hear you call for him or see where he is walking.

If your aging Akita has both hearing and vision loss, be patient with him. He will likely respond to physical cues, such as light pressure on his bottom when you need him to sit. However, this is not the time of his life to be teaching new commands - at this age, focus on spending quality time together!

Apart from the gradual decline of a dog's senses, there are other diseases that are more common in old age. Heart disease is somewhat common in aging dogs and may require special care. If you take your dog to regular vet visits, they will notice changes in your dog's heartbeat and can make recommendations. For some conditions, like a heart murmur, there may not be much you can do, but you should have your vet monitor all changes anyway.

You may also notice your dog slowing down because of poor cardiovascular health. Antioxidant supplements are a popular treatment for heart disease in dogs, and your vet may recommend such supplements.

Cancer is another issue with older dogs. When you pet your Akita, you may notice bumps under their skin. It is always a good idea to get these bumps and lumps checked out. Sometimes, dogs get benign tumors that do not affect your dog's health. Other times, they can be malignant and need to be removed. Then, a dog with cancer may require treatment to eliminate the cancerous cells from his body.

Senior dogs also tend to have issues with their kidneys and bladder and can experience incontinence. Since some medications can cause kidney disease, your vet will want to monitor your dog closely if he is taking medication in his advanced age. Blood tests can monitor your dog's kidney function over time.

Accidents in the house can be a sign of dementia or weakened muscles, but it can also be a sign of a urinary tract infection that can make a dog seriously ill if not treated immediately. If your dog is suddenly having accidents in the house, visit the vet to rule out serious causes.

Your aging Akita may have new health challenges, but he is still your best friend...that is something that never changes! Keep a close eye on any health or behavior changes. You may want to make more frequent appointments for checkups, as an aging dog's health can change rapidly, especially if your dog is on medication. Most importantly, make sure your Akita feels loved by spending quality time with him. Remember that your dog still needs stimulation and entertainment. Modified exercise and play will keep your dog sharp and happy during his final years.

FUN FACT
Akitas of Instagram

With over 59,000 followers, the Instagram account @akitasofinstagram is a fantastic place to see some adorable pictures of this breed. This account features photos of Akitas from the general community and might be one of the cutest places on the internet.

When It's Time to Say Goodbye

It can be heartbreaking to realize your dog is not living the quality of life he deserves. When your dog is well into his senior years, he will likely show a steep decline in overall health. At this point, an owner is faced with a tough decision: no one wants to say goodbye to their best friend, but sometimes, euthanasia is the kindest option for the end of your dog's life. You may know the time to make a decision is near if your dog is completely incontinent and his behavior suggests his mental and physical health is in decline.

Another sign is if your Akita is unable to move or is in obvious pain when he tries to move. Dogs tend to mask symptoms, so a dog that appears to be in pain is probably hurting badly. Also, a dog that cannot get up to eat or go to the bathroom will become sicker because he is not receiving proper nutrition or good hygiene. End-of-life decisions should be made when it is in the dog's best interest to end his life, not when advanced care becomes an inconvenience to the owner.

Photo Courtesy of Katie Russell

While some medical conditions that occur in old age - like blindness - are not serious enough to consider euthanasia, others like cancer or incontinence, may be a sign that your dog is in too much pain to continue living. Of course, you may choose to treat cancer if the vet believes surgery or medication can extend your dog's years in a humane way. Sometimes, surgery is too risky for an old and sick dog, and some types of treatment can make a dog feel weaker. Many owners will do what they can to prolong their dog's life, but advanced age and ill health can make it difficult to see positive results. A dog's body can only handle so much wear and tear, especially if he has prior conditions that are worsened by old age.

Sometimes, a dog appears to be at the end of his rope, but a new medication extends his quality of life for another year. Your vet has a lot of experience dealing with these matters and can help you make a decision. Understand, however, that a vet cannot make the choice for you - you can ask for advice, but ultimately, it is your choice.

When the day comes, your vet will offer you the option to stay in the room or to leave. While it can be extremely hard to witness a pet die, your Akita will be comforted by your presence during the painless procedure. If your dog was ever nervous at the vet, he will not want you to leave his side.

The dog will get an injection of a powerful sedative and will gently go to sleep. The euthanasia medicine will cause the dog's heart to stop beating within a short moment; the dog will not feel any pain during this quick process and might feel relieved. Apart from slight apprehension from being at the vet and the quick pinch of the needle, this process is not painful or scary to a dog. Even then, your dog may be too tired to feel nervous and will just be glad to have an owner who cares about him.

The mourning process after a beloved dog's death can be difficult for the entire family. Many vet clinics are willing to return the cremains to the owner and to offer special urns and memorials. Laws about burying pets vary from location to location so check your local laws or ask a vet before making a decision about burials.

However, there are other ways to memorialize your beloved Akita, even if his body is not physically with you. You may choose to keep pictures around your home or buy stuffed animal Akitas to remind you of your dog. It might also feel good to donate to an animal shelter or to an Akita rescue in memory of your dog. If you are not ready for a new pet but miss spending time around dogs, volunteer at a shelter or help a neighbor by walking their dogs.

When you're ready, take some time to find your next best friend. Do not rush into replacing a dog because you want to be distracted from the pain; you may find a new dog does not replace the emotions you are feeling.

Of course, a new dog will never truly replace your beloved Akita in your heart, but that does not mean you should never find a new dog to love. Consider volunteering with dogs or dog-sitting to get your puppy-fix before you are ready to begin the journey with a new Akita.

Made in the USA
Columbia, SC
07 January 2022